Arthur Gay Payne

Common-sense papers on Cookery

Arthur Gay Payne

Common-sense papers on Cookery

ISBN/EAN: 9783744789868

Printed in Europe, USA, Canada, Australia, Japan

Cover: Foto ©Andreas Hilbeck / pixelio.de

More available books at **www.hansebooks.com**

COMMON-SENSE PAPERS

ON

COOKERY.

BY

A. G. PAYNE.

CASSELL PETTER & GALPIN:
London, Paris & New York.

PREFACE.

THE present work has no pretensions to be a complete book on Cooking, but is simply a series of papers (which originally appeared in CASSELL'S MAGAZINE) in which the endeavour has been, to impart a certain amount of useful knowledge of the Art of Cooking, by giving recipes at greater length than would be possible in any ordinary Cookery Book.

Ordinary Cookery Books, though of the greatest utility, are, like dictionaries, seldom if ever read through. In the present work, which contains all the important elements and first principles of Cookery necessary to be learnt, in order to render ordinary works on the subject intelligible, the attempt has been made to so mingle recipes with anecdote, that the perusal of the book may be a means of entertainment as well as of useful information.

The work is intended more for the drawing-room than for the kitchen, for the Author believes that, among the great mass of the middle classes in this country—the class that is suffering most from the incapacity of domestic servants—the remedy lies with themselves.

A helpless mistress too often makes helpless servants. It is in the hope of curing some of this wide-spread helplessness amongst ladies that the following papers have been written.

CONTENTS.

		PAGE
I.—Uses and Abuses of a Frying-Pan	. . .	9
II.—Kitchen Economy	.	22
III.—Little Extravagancies of the Table	. .	32
IV.—Cold Leg of Mutton . . .	. .	43
V.—How to make Dishes look nice .	. .	56
VI.—Breakfast Dishes . . .	. .	68
VII.—How to give a nice little Dinner .	. .	79
VIII.—How to give a nice little Supper	. .	93
IX.—Spring Dishes	. .	104
X.—Savoury Summer Dishes . .	. .	114
XI.—Salads, and how to make them .	. .	127
XII.—Picnic Dainties . . .	. .	138
XIII.—Cooling Drinks . . .	. .	149
XIV.—Game and Gravy (including How to Cook Hare)		160
XV.—Food for Cold Weather . .	. .	182
XVI.—Christmas Dinners (including Christmas Cheer)	.	191
XVII.—Turtle Soup . . .	. .	209
XVIII.—Fish Dinners . . .	. .	221
XIX.—Wedding Breakfasts . .	. .	233
XX.—Food for Invalids . .	. .	241

COMMON-SENSE PAPERS ON COOKERY.

I.—THE USES AND ABUSES OF A FRYING-PAN.

"We had such an awful time of it with Mary Ann!" Probably, never have the domestic trials and difficulties of young housekeepers been summed up in fewer or more expressive words. However, the more we look into the world, the more we find it to be the case that we make our Mary Anns, and not our Mary Anns us.

It is a good old saying that the master makes the man; equally true is it that the mistress makes the maid. Let each of our readers pause for an instant, and look round mentally among his relations and friends with whom he is in the habit of dining. Each one, probably, has had many changes of servants, yet there are some houses where the dinner is invariably good, others where it is equally invariably bad. Who has not, on entering a house where he expects to dine, been greeted at the door with a whiff of the smell of the cooking, from which whiff he could pretty well determine in his own mind the style of dinner he may expect?

No cooking is so good as the French, none so bad as a certain style of English. Compare the smell of a good French restaurant, or outside the kitchen of a first-class hotel, like the "Pavilion" at Folkestone, an hour before the table d'hôte, with the smell of an ordinary cook-shop, with its steam-pipes keeping warm large flabby joints and greasy Yorkshire pudding, the whole being impregnated with that peculiar smell of greens in which one can almost fancy he detects the flavour of caterpillars.

I think it may be laid down as a rule that if, on entering a house, you smell greens, you may make up your mind for a bad dinner. On the other hand, a gamey smell, with perhaps just a dash of garlic in it, is favourable, especially if mingled with the smell of rich pastry.

It would, however, require many volumes to enter into a minute description of a good and a bad dinner. We would rather be practical, and, if possible, useful.

The natural resource of young housekeepers is the cookery-book. After the pathetic statement with which our article commences, David Copperfield proceeds as follows :—

"In search of the principle on which joints ought to be roasted—to be roasted enough and not too much—I myself referred to the cookery-book, and found it there established as the allowance of a quarter of an hour to every pound, and say a quarter over. But the principle always failed us by some curious fatality, and we never could hit any medium between redness and cinders."

Here is the old story, and one that, probably, happens every day, and will happen—viz., reference to a cookery-book; the directions followed; the result—failure. Who is most to blame—the cook, or the book?

That the book is often in fault there can be no doubt. So long as we meet with such absurdities as "and flavour to taste," or "add seasoning," &c., we shall continue to maintain that recipes that contain these directions might just as well have never been written.

But in the present article we wish to confine ourselves to the "frying-pan," one of the most useful, and, at the same time, abused articles of kitchen use.

We will suppose that a certain dish consists of something fried. Perhaps one or two are expected to dinner who are known or supposed to be rather particular. The mistress has consulted the cookery-book, which gravely recommends as follows:—"Fry of a nice golden-colour, and serve hot." How to do it, however, we are not informed. Suppose the dish to be a fried sole or a sweetbread. We all know the real thing—a sweetbread at the Café Bignon—soft and white inside, and a perfect golden-brown out, without even a shade of colour varying in the whole dish. On the other hand, a sweetbread *à la* Mary Ann, covered with bread-crumbs, some a whitey-brown, some brown, and some black, but still containing patches with no bread-crumbs at all, looking like a cat's back where the cook had accidentally spilt some boiling water.

Or, perhaps, a still greater blunder has been made. On this particular occasion Mary Ann, who means well, endeavours to do her utmost to make things *look* nice, and in trying to obtain this nice golden-colour, fries the sole till it is so dried up that it becomes scarcely eatable. Who has not occasionally in small families noticed the slight passing shadow of annoyance on the face of the hostess, as she becomes aware of some such little *contretemps?*—in which, perhaps, a very close observer of human nature might detect the thought: " It will never warm up for breakfast."

Now, is it possible to write clear directions, so that any one with an average amount of common sense can, by following them, fry fish, sweetbreads, &c., which will combine colour with quality? We believe it is possible; at any rate, it is worth the attempt.

All fish that has to be fried with egg and bread-crumbs must be treated alike in this respect. The fish must first be thoroughly dried. Next, it must be floured. This is done in order to ensure its being dry, just as a baby's neck is powdered for a similar purpose after being dried with a towel. Next, the egg must be thoroughly beaten up before it is used; otherwise, the white of the egg especially is apt to slip off, leaving those bald patches we have mentioned. Again, the bread-crumbs must be dry and fine. It is no use to attempt to use bread-crumbs made from new bread, which will be necessarily coarse.

Now, we will suppose these conditions complied with—say a sole has been carefully dried and floured, has been carefully egged over, and then covered with some very fine bread-crumbs. Most cooks will say: "Well, then fry it in plenty of hot fat, allow it to drain on a napkin, and that's all."

Wait a minute. If you have a frying-pan two feet in diameter, filled with boiling fat three inches deep, this would do very well. A few minutes would suffice to cook the sole a nice colour, "all over alike." But have you this? Probably, to start with, the fish is a trifle longer than the frying-pan. The fat is a quarter of an inch deep, and won't cover the fish. How, under these very common circumstances, will you get your fish to look nice?

Go to the baker's at once, and order in as follows (it does not cost anything)—a bag of light-brown bread-raspings, of about the colour you would use for a ham. Always have some by you—they keep almost for ever, and, as I have said, the baker gives them away. Take some of these, and make them fine—a rolling-pin and a little patience are sufficient for the purpose. Take these fine raspings and sprinkle the sole—we left it egged and bread-crumbed well on both sides—lo, and behold! the sole, even before it is put in the frying-pan, is all that is desirable in the way of colour. The weight is off your mind; all you now have to do is to cook it so that it is done through without being dried up.

Now for this purpose you must have a certain depth of lard or dripping, or it cannot be done. Properly speaking, there ought to be enough fat to cover the fish. However, it is no use writing for things as they ought to be; it is more practical to write for things as they are. You must have enough fat at least to dip the sole in. Of course it is impossible to draw any exact line between a single drop of fat and a gallon. What we mean is, it is no use to try and fry fish in a frying-pan that has had a little piece of butter put in it, just sufficient to prevent the fish from sticking. A properly fried fish is one which has been boiled in fat.

If, therefore, you have not sufficient to cover the sole, it will be necessary to cook one side first, and then the other. With regard to the time it takes, this of course, altogether depends on the thickness of the fish. If you have enough fat to cover the fish, the very largest sole would not take more than ten minutes. The mistake generally made in frying fish is to over-cook it. A properly fried sole must appear moist inside on lifting the meat from the bone. Still, the meat must not stick to the bone, or look red. However, with regard to time, experience alone will teach, but recollect an under-cooked fish can always be warmed up, and an over-cooked one—never. Besides, a beginner can lift the fish off the fire after a few minutes, take a knife, and look at the meat nearest the bone in the thickest part. If it is white, and not transparent, it is done enough, and a pinch of raspings hides the place. With a cook, however, of almost any experience, this is unnecessary.

Another exceedingly important point is, the fat must be boiling. This can generally be found out by dropping a single drop of cold water into it, and if it makes a great hiss, the fat boils. On dipping the fish into the fat, a noise ought to ensue somewhat similar to that made by plunging a red-hot poker into a pail of water.

When the fish is done, lift it on to a hot cloth, in

order to let the fat drain off it, keeping it of course in front of the fire, and afterwards lift the fish carefully, and without breaking it, on to a clean napkin folded in a dish, or over a strainer made for the purpose.

Now some of these directions may seem unnecessary, on account of their being so very obvious. But then it must be borne in mind that there are Mary Anns whose stupidity is absolutely unfathomable. I recollect, many years ago, being in lodgings at the sea-side—it was at Worthing—where I met two specimens in the shape of mistress and servant that would, I think, match any pair ever likely to come together again. The mistress, who was also cook, seemed to require a considerable amount of stimulant, and under its influence the following scraps of conversation could be heard at intervals throughout the day :—

"Please, mum, where's the rolling-pin?"

"I'll rolling-pin yer!"

On asking whether there were any eggs, the unfortunate girl said—

"I think there's some in the cupboard," which called forth—

"Now, Mary Ann, what do you mean by thinking? never let me hear you think again."

The climax in the way of cooking was a fruit pie, as the handmaiden informed us—

"Please, sir, missus is very sorry, but she forgot the butter."

The pastry, as may be imagined, was not what may be called light; however, the crust came off as a lid, and we amused ourselves by spinning it like a teetotum. Of course such cases are exceptional, but I have known a grouse stuffed with sage and onion. On another occasion a couple were sent to a farmer's wife to be got ready for lunch. This was adjoining the moor where they were shot. The party to their astonishment found them boiled.

While the fish is draining is a good opportunity to fry a little parsley to put round it. All that is required is fresh, clean parsley—dry. A minute is sufficient to leave it in the fat, if the fat boils. Take out the parsley with a slice, and let it dry on the cloth by the side of the fish. It will soon become crisp. A large wire slice will be found better than an ordinary one.

If the fish has been large, and the frying-pan rather small, it is quite possible that in turning the fish a little of the bread-crumbs may get knocked off, though with care this ought not to be the case. When, however, it is, you can always mend the patch with a pinch of raspings.

Now, the greatest difficulty in following these directions will probably be found to be "the quantity of fat." It is always a sore point with the cooks. They look upon fat as one of their perquisites, and too often the mistress will find that she has to be constantly ordering in a skin of lard, or has to order dripping, in order to fry fish.

Recollect, however, that the same fat will do to fry fish over and over again—though it should be kept entirely for fish—and that it will often keep for months. Cooks are too fond, from interested motives, of making it out bad. It will be found in small families an excellent rule to forbid fat and grease being sold at all. Were ladies to insist on this, which they could always do with young servants, much mischief would be avoided. Selling dripping and candle-grease is often the thin end of the wedge to downright theft. The class of people who buy are too often little better than receivers of stolen property, and sometimes lead young servants into small acts of dishonesty, in order to get them in their power, the consequence of which is that small acts are followed by great.

In frying sweetbreads it should be borne in mind that the sweetbreads should be soaked some hours in water first, and then boiled for about five or ten minutes, according to their size, and placed in cold water to get cold. When cold they should be carefully dried, and egged and bread-crumbed like the fish, and then covered over with the bread-raspings, to ensure their being of a good and equal colour. Should the fat not be sufficient to cover them, they must be turned occasionally in the frying-pan. The fat, as before, must boil before they are put in. Tomato or rich brown sauce can be poured round them, or served separately, but should not be poured over them, as they should possess a dry golden-brown colour.

We have now described some of the uses of the frying-pan, and have given an instance of both a thick and thin substance for frying; but what are its abuses? Cooks are very apt to use the frying-pan for what they ought not. Too often they will use it instead of the gridiron to cook a chop or a steak, and if there is one thing in the world utterly spoilt in the cooking, it is a good rump steak cooked in a frying-pan. Yet it will often be found, even in decent houses, that chops and steaks, especially the former, are cooked in this manner. A dish of chops appears, perhaps at lunch, the dish swimming in gravy, in which can clearly be tasted the ketchup that has been added. After a few minutes the gravy will be seen to be studded with blotches of grease about the size of wafers. The chops taste greasy and sodden, and the roof of the mouth becomes soon coated with hard mutton-fat.

How different to a chop properly cooked on a

gridiron! Black outside, red in, and brought up on a hot plate, on to which about a tea-spoonful of clear red gravy may have run. The first mouthful you take ought to burn your mouth. Such is a mutton chop as it ought to be; and there are often times when an invalid or a person of delicate appetite feels as if there is nothing else he can eat. It, however, requires a tolerably thick gridiron, a clear fire, and common sense.

A singular instance of audacity in the way of cooking a steak occurred at a country inn where we were once unfortunate enough to try and dine.

The waiter was a model of a dirty man in the right place. Everything was in unison—table-cloth, forks, wine-glasses, and thumb-nails to match. He might have been the original for that admirable little sketch in *Punch*, where the elderly gentleman exclaims, "Why, confound you! you are wiping my plate with your pocket-handkerchief!"—the reply being, "Oh, it's of no consequence, sir; it's only a dirty one!"

We had a steak, the cooking of which completely baffled us. What possible method was adopted to make it what it was, we could not conceive. We made friends with the dirty man, and in time extracted the information that the cook always boiled the chops and steaks for a few minutes, previous to browning them in a frying-pan. This, the waiter informed me, was a capital thing for the soup.

We have endeavoured to explain the art of frying at greater length than it would be possible to do in any work on cooking, and on some future occasion may again call attention to some of the points where ordinary books on the subject seem to us to fail to meet the requirements of small households. Unfortunately, many of the best works on cooking are only adapted for very large establishments, or hotels, where probably a book would not be required.

For instance, a recipe for Yorkshire pie, as given in one of the best works on cooking yet published, commences as follows :—" First bone a turkey, a goose, a brace of pheasants, four partridges, a dozen snipes, four grouse, and four widgeons ; then boil and trim a small York ham and two tongues," &c. The recipe, we have no doubt, is excellent, but with all due submission to so great an authority, it appears scarcely adapted for small families of limited income.

II.—KITCHEN ECONOMY.

There is perhaps no word so little understood, or rather so misunderstood, as the word "economy." Just as there is a vulgar and popular impression that political economists are a hard-hearted, selfish class, so domestic economy is too often regarded as a synonymous term for meanness and want of hospitality. Conversely, too many are apt to confound extravagance with liberality. Economy in regard to money has been defined as "the judicious use of money." So in cooking economy simply means the judicious use of materials. In fact, economy is closely allied to common-sense, whereas extravagance is the twin sister of ignorance. Good cooks are never wasteful. The difference between a good dish and a bad one often consists simply in the fact that in the one all the flavour has been extracted from the materials used; in the other, part—often the best part—has been lost and thrown away. Nowhere is waste and extravagance so wanton and reckless as among the extreme poor, and the more ignorant the worse they are. The savage method of cooking roast pork illustrates our point. As savages are more ignorant even than the lowest of our own lower orders, we ought to expect to find them more extravagant and reckless. Such is the case. On one occasion an Indian wigwam or hut, containing a live pig, caught fire. After the fire had subsided, and the embers were raked away, the remains of the unfortunate animal were found inside, which on being tasted proved to be far superior to the raw flesh to which the Indians were accustomed. Consequently, on great occasions, when a dish of roast pork is required, it has been the custom ever since to drive a pig into some small hut or house, and then set the house on fire. Now, this method has all the charm of simplicity, but still it is not altogether an economical method; though there are some dens and hovels even in this country where no one could regret the experiment.

But to take a simple case to illustrate our point, we will describe that very common sauce, lobster sauce, and contrast it as it is with what it ought to be, trusting that our description of the latter will be attended with the practical result of enabling those who read it to make it for themselves, should they so desire, besides something in addition.

First, we all know the lobster sauce which too often is handed round as an accompaniment to some boiled fish, such as turbot or brill. It consists simply of melted butter, with small pieces of lobster—some white, some pink—cut up in it; but as to the liquid sauce itself, it does not contain even the slightest flavour of lobster whatever. On the other hand, good lobster sauce is of a bright red colour, and tasting so strongly of lobster that it is too often apt to entirely overpower the flavour of the fish. Yet this latter has probably been made out of exactly the same materials as the former. What, then, is the difference? Simply this :—In the one case all the flavour of the lobster has been extracted, and in the other it has not. Cutting up the meat of a lobster and putting the pieces into melted butter is no more making lobster sauce than cutting up a calf's head and throwing the pieces into boiling water would be making mock-turtle soup.

We will suppose, now, the very ordinary case of some lobster sauce being required for a small party, say eight persons; the ordinary method being for a lobster to be ordered, the white part of the meat cut up and put into some melted butter, while the pickings, so called, generally make a tit-bit at the kitchen supper, with the usual accompaniment of at least a pint of vinegar. Now, what is the difficulty? First, even a small lobster is amply sufficient to supply sauce for double the number. Every one who has eyes, and knows how to use them, must have observed how invariably it is the case that in small households fish sauce of any description is always made in gigantic proportions. We have seen melted butter of the consistency of a pudding brought up for four persons, in quantity sufficient for the table d'hôte at the Grand Hotel in Paris. Make up your mind, therefore, as follows :—Order a moderate-sized lobster, and have a dish of lobster cutlets as an entreé in addition to the sauce for the fish.

Now, there are few prettier dishes than lobster cutlets, and few easier to make, yet how rarely is it met with in small households !

First, get a lobster containing some spawn and coral. Cut open the lobster and remove the whole of the meat, including that in the claws, and cut it up into small pieces, and put it on a plate and place it in a cool place, to be used as we shall explain by-and-by. Next take the spawn and coral and place it in a mortar with about twice the quantity of butter, and pound it well together, adding a good pinch of cayenne pepper. You will by this means obtain what is called lobster butter, and without it it is impossible to make either good lobster sauce, or patties, or cutlets, or bisque—the latter being, in other words, lobster soup.

This lobster butter has a strong lobster flavour, and is of an exceedingly brilliant colour. It will keep a long time, and good cooks should always try and have some by them, as ofttimes lobsters contain neither spawn or coral. Scrape all the lobster butter out of the mortar, and place it in some small jar for use. Next (we are supposing that eight persons are the number at dinner), take about a dessert-spoonful of the cut-up meat and put it by for the sauce—this quantity will be amply sufficient—and take all the rest of the meat and place it in a mortar, and pound it up with the following materials, previously chopped *very* fine: a piece of onion as big as the top of the thumb down to the bottom of the nail, a small tea-spoonful of chopped parsley, and a piece of lemon-peel the size and thickness of the thumb-nail. But while these are being pounded, let us return to and finish making the lobster sauce. First, make a little rather thin melted butter, using milk instead of water; add sufficient lobster butter to make it a bright red colour, this lobster butter containing as a rule sufficient cayenne pepper for the whole sauce. Add the dessert-spoonful of lobster meat, about half a salt-spoonful of anchovy sauce, and the same quantity of lemon-juice, and the sauce is complete. The quantity of melted butter made should be regulated by the size of the ladle in the sauce-tureen. There are over twelve ordinary ladlefuls in half a pint; as a rule each person takes one ladleful, therefore half a pint of lobster sauce is more than sufficient for eight persons. If you don't want waste, tell your cook to pour a tumblerful of water into a sauce-tureen, and see how much it looks, and never to make more melted butter for eight or even ten persons. The melted butter should not be made, however, until it is nearly dinner-time, as *properly*-made melted butter is apt to decompose or run oily if exposed to heat too long.

And now, let us return to the rest of the lobster, which we left being pounded in the mortar, and to which have been added the chopped onion, parsley, and lemon-peel in the proportions we have mentioned. Mix in sufficient lobster butter to make the whole mass appear of a bright-red colour—about a brimming tea-spoonful is generally sufficient to a medium-sized lobster. After this add some ordinary butter—about two ounces—but, of course, the quantity must vary with the size and meatiness of the lobster, but sufficient must be added to make the whole quantity into a sort of thick pudding, which when struck with a table-spoon makes a noise like—slosh.

Next mould the mass into a quantity of small pieces, the size and shape of an oval pic-nic biscuit. This moulding is best done with the hands, by throwing the piece from one palm into the other. Dip each piece in a well-beaten-up egg—of course, one egg is sufficient for the whole quantity—and then into some fine dry bread-crumbs. Fry in some *boiling* fat or lard for about two minutes, and put each piece on a cloth to drain for a few minutes in front of the fire.

Stick a small piece of the end of the small claws of the lobster—say about three-quarters of an inch long—into each, to represent the bone of the cutlet, and the dish is complete, though it had better be put into the oven for four or five minutes just before serving.

When lobsters are cheap, the cost of these pretty little red cutlets varies from one penny to three-halfpence each. I once made twenty from a lobster that cost one shilling and sixpence. There are many ignorant people, who on seeing such a dish would imagine that it must be a very extravagant one; and yet these same persons would think nothing of having a dish of six or eight ordinary mutton cutlets handed round as an entrée, costing at least sixpence each. Besides, there is no comparison in the appearance of the two dishes. There are, perhaps, few entrées more invariably passed by at dinner-parties than mutton cutlets, unless dressed ones, which, especially when truffles are used, are very expensive. A dish of bright-red lobster cutlets, neatly arranged in a silver dish, with a pile of crisp fried parsley in the centre, always looks nice; and if economy is very much thought of, a few bread-crumbs added to the mass before moulding will increase the dish, but we don't recommend the method: we wish to be practical: and the probable result of the suggestion to the cook is that the cutlets will be spoilt, and the cook will have the best claw for her supper, served *au naturel*--*i.e.*, with the vinegar aforesaid.

It seems very dreadful, when one comes to think about it, but how horribly dependent we all are upon our servants! and, as a rule, how far less regard have they to economy than we have ourselves! This is probably owing to early education—for instance, the girl who in childhood has been accustomed to see her mother buy coals by the apronful. Yes, gentle reader, such is the fact, which you may see for yourself any day in some of the poorer neighbourhoods in London. I recollect a case once in which the apron-strings gave way, thereby causing the coal-cellar to make a sudden and unexpected appearance on the pavement, and calling forth the exclamation of—

"Drat the thing!"

Yet this very girl, who, as we said, has been used to see her mother lay in coals in this fashion, when she goes out to service is so overcome by the inexhaustible supply, as it seems to her, in a cellar containing several tons, that from sheer thoughtlessness she is extravagant to a degree. In most houses the ashes are thrown up far more often in the dining-room than in the kitchen.

Another and ofttimes a more terrible difficulty that young housekeepers have to contend with, is the impenetrable stupidity of the women in her employ. I recollect a most amusing case that occurred many years ago in a house at Woolwich. An elderly lady—one of the good old sort, not above occasional interference in domestic matters—had personally superintended the preparation of that somewhat nasty creature in the raw state, a hare for jugging. The richest of gravy had been prepared, the joints of the hare had been neatly browned in a frying-pan without being cooked. Cloves, port wine, &c.—nothing had been forgotten, and the whole had been placed in a large jug, and only required being put to simmer gently in some boiling water. Now, the elderly lady wisely thought that the copper would be as safe a place as any wherein to stand the jug, the water reaching about half-way up, this method having the additional advantage of leaving more room on the kitchen fire, besides obviating the risk of its being upset by the saucepan—if the jug were placed in one—being hastily moved. Directions were given accordingly.

Imagine the elderly lady's face on discovering, about a quarter of an hour before dinner, that Mary Ann had put the jug in the copper by simply emptying it in!

But I fear I have rather got away from my subject, which is that of economy. Now, economy is the very soul of cookery, and can be alike practised in the palace and the cottage, and, unfortunately, is less regarded in the latter than in the former. It is wonderful how many really nice dishes may be made out of odds and ends. In a well-managed house there ought not to be enough left to keep even a dog; whereas, if the truth were known, the contents of the dust-bins alone in England contain sufficient food to almost banish poverty from the land. This may seem a strong statement, but it is no more strong than true. Recollect waste is a crime; and were it in our power —which it is not—to be able to multiply food even to a miraculous extent, it would not the less be our duty to "gather up the fragments that remain, that nothing be lost."

III.—LITTLE EXTRAVAGANCIES OF THE TABLE.

The importance of such a subject as the one I have now taken in hand is apt to be much underrated. Many a starving family could be fed from the wasted superabundance which falls, in too many cases, not only from the rich man's, but the comparatively poor man's table.

There is no extravagance so disastrous as the extravagance of ignorance. It is perhaps as difficult to define precisely where hospitality and comfort end, and extravagance begins, as it is to define where economy ends and meanness begins. Strange to say, however, we not unfrequently find extravagance and meanness go hand in hand. How often do we find households conducted upon inconsistent principles! For instance, a fine large house, dogs, horses, and carriages, and yet one cannot get a good glass of sherry at dinner, or any wine at all after. Rows of fine greenhouses as well as hot-houses, full of rare plants, and no fire in the bedroom. I sometimes think that quite the poor are a great deal better off than the rich for real luxuries.

I know I have stopped at some houses, and thought with a sigh of the poor man's, with the feather bed, especially when the blankets are out of pawn. After all, happiness is much more equally distributed in the world than some people think for, and living in one room has its advantages as well as its drawbacks. The pennyworth of fried fish warmed up in the oven, with appetite sauce, will hold its own with the best of *vols-au-vent* without. But all this has very little to do with the subject, which is not household management in general, but table extravagance in particular.

Perhaps the most common form of extravagance is profusion, which is very marked in certain dishes; and we before called attention to melted butter, which is invariably made in quantity sufficient for quite ten times the number at dinner. Fish is commonly supplied in quantity enough for double the number; for instance, three or four persons do not want a pair of large soles; one would be ample, and the other would do for breakfast cooked fresh; instead, it is either warmed up and spoilt, or eaten cold at the servants' supper with a knife and vinegar. Another form of extravagance is cooking too many potatoes every day regularly. I know one or two houses where more than half the dish of potatoes has been left every day for the last twenty years, and I feel confident will continue to be left for twenty years to come. Again,

c

some servants invariably cut up a great deal more bread for dinner than is necessary, the stale pieces left too often finding their way into the pig-tub. Speaking of pig-tubs reminds me of a little incident that came to my knowledge only last Christmas. A gentleman living in a country village kept one pig, and had been in the habit of paying 1s. a week for grains from the brewery. His gardener, who lived in a little cottage a mile off, and kept pigs of his own, informed him that he was in the habit of buying pig-wash from the cooks in the neighbourhood, to whom he paid 1s. a month, and suggested that he should receive the 1s. a week, and in return find the wash, guaranteeing the pig would thrive far better. The first pail of wash the man brought to the house ought indeed to be a caution to housekeepers, containing as it did large lumps of bread, whole cooked potatoes, and chicken-bones half-picked.

The gentleman, who is my own brother, declared to me that he had seen pails of pig-wash containing broken victuals sufficient to keep a poor family for a week, and jokingly remarked that should he ever be really hard up, he should dine at his pig's. These facts, however, are no joke. I believe the extravagance of ignorant servants, in large households where the mistress does not enter into domestic affairs, is beyond all conception. As Sam Weller observes, if some servants got their deserts it would be very little cold swarry they would ever eat again. I have known cases where a jug of beer left from a late dinner has been poured down the sink, and some fresh beer drawn for the kitchen supper, on the ground that the beer left would taste flat.

Some joints are undoubtedly more extravagant than others. I wonder what a French cook thinks of the English roast loin of mutton. The bones are always left half-picked on the plate, and too often the end left altogether, besides which the roast loin of mutton seems to possess the unamiable property of getting cold sooner than any other joint I know of.

Now, bone the joint, and stuff it with veal stuffing; the raw bones will of course make soup, and nothing is wasted.

It is always extravagant to use up any joint or poultry, when it can be helped, when bones are left on the plates. I succeeded some little time ago in persuading a shockingly bad housekeeper not to bring up the remains of a large turkey cold. It was treated instead as follows:—With the assistance of a small tin of mushrooms, part of it made some Russian Kromeskies; another part made a dish of mince; some nice slices cut off the remains of the breast were converted into a capital Mayonnaise; while the two legs—for it was a fine bird, weighing twenty-one pounds—were devilled, and sent up with some devil sauce, which I may briefly describe as follows :—Cut up some young onions very fine, and moisten them with a very little French vinegar, and boil for about five or six minutes ; add some cayenne pepper, some good strong gravy, wine, and anchovy butter, which latter consists of filleted anchovies pounded very thoroughly in a mortar with some butter and cayenne.

Any grilled meat, such as a chop, or drumsticks of fowls, is very much improved by a sauce of this kind. Of course, the cayenne must be suited in quantity to the tastes of the eaters. But to return to the turkey : by treating it in the manner I have described, there was no waste, all the bones being saved, and the result was that they made more than half a gallon of stock, which when cold was a hard jelly.

Another common form of waste is home-made pastry. I recollect some oyster patties as they were called, but oyster pies as they really were, being very nearly as big as cheese-plates, in which the pastry was so out of proportion to the oyster that the dish was almost ludicrous, the impossibility of eating even a quarter of the pastry being self-evident the moment the pie was cut. I have seen lobster patties made on a similar principle, in which, when the top was taken off, the lobster part appeared beneath, something not merely in colour, but in size resembling a red wafer. Now these dishes are really very extravagant, for the reason that they cost both money and trouble, and in the end no one eats them.

A somewhat eccentric form of the "extravagance of ignorance" to which I have alluded, is that of warming up joints that have been not only cooked before, but cut. In the first place, if the joint is cooked properly the first day, every one possessing even the vestige of a palate would surely prefer it cold to being warmed up and spoilt. The probable reason of warming up a joint a second day is that the cook knows of no other way of extricating herself from the difficulty of sending up cold meat. Such extreme ignorance is, however, I am pleased to say, rare. I once knew a case of a loin of mutton which went through the following awful processes:—First it was roasted, fortunately being a trifle blue; the second day it was roasted again, the flavour being of course quite gone. The awful part remains behind—the rest was cut into chops, egged and bread-crumbed, and sent up as cutlets; and I, alas! ate one.

Another instance of waste and extravagance is a ham which is allowed to get musty. It will be found that a ham when it first comes up is very popular, but wait till the middle bone is distinctly visible, and the fat has a yellow tinge and doubtful smell—no one will touch it. But why let it go so far? Why not pot it? Potted ham is easily made, will keep a long time, and is always useful. Now, to pot ham, take a pound of the lean to half a pound of the fat, or less—in fact, a pound of lean to a quarter of fat does even better for potting—mince it very fine, or, better still, run it through a sausage-machine, and add to, say the pound and a half, a small tea-spoonful of pounded mace, about a quarter of a good-sized nutmeg, grated, of course, and about a salt-spoonful of cayenne pepper. Less mace may be used, or a little pounded allspice added instead; one dried bay-leaf powdered may be added also.

Mix all this up thoroughly, and press it down in the dish or pot in which it will be served. Bake it in the oven for about twenty-five minutes, taking care the top does not brown, and then press it down very hard—a weight is a good thing to use for the purpose—and cover the top with some fresh lard, which must be first melted, and then poured on the top. Ham potted this way will keep good for months. Fresh clarified butter may be used, but lard is best, especially in summer.

One very common form of extravagance, which is essentially the extravagance of ignorance, is giving the cook orders for certain dishes without ascertaining whether the materials are in season or not. I recollect hearing, some time ago, of a married couple living in London, who, liking a little fish every day for dinner, made a contract with the fishmonger to send each day, about six o'clock, what fish suited him best; I believe they paid regularly 6d. a day. It is on such principles that tables-d'hôte can be given so cheaply at hotels. The manager of the hotel goes to market and buys—especially in fish—what happens to be plentiful. Good wholesome fish may be bought in Billingsgate Market sometimes at a penny a pound.

Let me now endeavour to tell you how to make mock-turtle soup out of pig's head, instead of calf's head. Now, calves' heads vary immensely in price; when half a head can be got for 2s. 6d. or 3s., it is a fairly economical dish; but when calves' heads, as happens sometimes about Christmas, owing to the extraordinary demand for them, run up to a guinea each, of course the dish would be extravagant to a degree. I don't know what the price of pigs' heads is in the country, but in London they can generally be bought for 6d. a pound. To make mock-turtle soup from, say half a head, first scald it thoroughly, then put it on to boil gently in some stock made from bones. The drawback to the soup is that it has a tendency to taste greasy, consequently the point to be always borne in mind is to thoroughly get rid of the fat. After the pig's head has boiled for about an hour and a half, take it out, let it get partially cold, then cut the meat off the head exactly in the same shape as the pieces of calf's head in good mock-turtle soup; let each piece be about an inch and a half or two inches square. These should be allowed to get cold between two large dishes, the bottom one being placed upside-down, as in cooling they have a tendency to curl, and they look far better flat. Put all the bones of the head back into the stock, and let them boil as long as you like. I would mention, in passing, that a couple of bay-leaves in the stock are a great improvement. Next thicken the stock with brown thickening, which is, as I have before described, simply flour fried brown in butter. Let the whole boil very gently, and keep skimming it carefully. It is surprising what a lot of fat there will be on it. This soup should always be made the day before it is wanted, in order to let it get cold; the fat can then be taken off, but I would warn cooks against supposing that because soup has got cold *all* the fat will necessarily float to the top, as this is not the case. A great deal of fat is what may be termed held in solution in the soup, and is only thrown up by boiling. When therefore all the fat has been got rid of, the pieces of meat can be replaced in the soup, and some sherry added—golden sherry, or, still better, madeira—and recollect that this latter wine is fairly cheap again now; as, therefore, you have saved money over the pig's head instead of the calf's head, you can afford to be a little more generous with the wine. It is wonderful what a difference this latter makes in the flavour; only just taste it for yourself before and after. Soup like this will bear a large claret-glass of sherry, or even more; only pray put in the wine yourself, for if your cook happens to "have a weakness that way," it may never be mingled with the soup at all.

I believe it to be real extravagance to buy things that are out of season, in addition to its being foolish. It will generally be found that things are nicest when cheapest; for instance, strawberries are never so good as when they can be bought for 6d. a basket. Who the people are that buy the peaches at 5s. each, pines at a guinea, and green peas at 10s. a pint, I cannot say, but that such people exist is evident from a walk through Covent Garden Market. Such sort of extravagance seems to me to be hardly consistent with good moral character. There is a story told of a lady who was particularly fond of the "Pope's eye" in a leg of mutton, and would often have a dozen legs ordered, simply for the sake of cutting out the "Pope's eyes," the rest of the meat being given to hounds. The story, however, sounds too wicked to be true.

I heard a delightful story, a short time ago, of an extravagant husband who was blessed, or cursed, as the case may be, with a wife who may be described as "a little near." In expectation of a dinner-party, which to him was a business dinner, expecting as he did some friends from the City, he ordered a salmon from his fishmonger, the price being £1. Fearing, however, that his better half would find fault with the price, and being anxious to prove himself good at a bargain, he paid down 10s., and sent home the fish as if the remaining 10s. was the whole charge. On his return, his wife, with great glee, told him how she had disposed of the fish to her friend Mrs. ———, who had called, seen the fish, and, thinking it remarkably cheap, had offered 15s. for it, which offer had been gladly accepted. The wretched man's feelings can be better imagined than described; but the moral of the story, which is really true, seems to be—Don't deceive your wife!

IV.—COLD LEG OF MUTTON.

A FEW years ago the leading comic journal of the day had the following graphic little sketch :—A middle-aged gentleman, leaving his house-door in the morning, inquires—

"What is there for dinner to-day, Mary?"

"Cold mutton, sir."

"Then you can tell your mistress that she need not wait dinner for me."

Now, although this sounds exceedingly selfish, yet perhaps the blame is not entirely due to one side only.

There can be no doubt that, just as among the lower orders there are hundreds of wives who, from ignorance and stupidity, drive their husbands to the public-house, so among the middle classes there are as many who from the same causes too often drive them to the "Club."

Now, the increase in the number of these luxurious establishments in the present day is something wonderful. It has already had a marked effect upon the restaurants in the metropolis, some of which now do not dine half what they did formerly ; but it remains to be seen how far the clubs will in time affect the Registrar-General's marriage-returns. As this latter point is of the greatest importance to that large and charming portion of the population, the young unmarried ladies, we trust we may be pardoned if for one moment we pause to ask them a few questions.

Did you ever consider how your future husband is accustomed to dine every day, and contrast it with the way in which he will dine when you will have the management of the household? We will suppose him to be accustomed to the ordinary club dinner, or say the regimental mess. Do you not feel how entirely dependent you will be on your cook? Should she be clever and honest, you may do very well. Should she, however, be idle and dishonest, what will you do?

Now do not, pray, think that to get a good common-sense cook is by any means an easy affair. If you only inquire of your friends and relations, you will soon find out the difficulty.

You have all probably read that exquisite little sketch in "David Copperfield," who mildly addresses his "child-wife" as follows:—" You must remember, I am sure, that I was obliged to go out yesterday when dinner was half-over, and that the day before I was made quite unwell by being obliged to eat underdone veal in a hurry; to-day I don't dine at all; and I am afraid to say how long we waited for breakfast, and then the water didn't boil. I don't mean to reproach you, my dear, but this is not comfortable."

Unfortunately, this is only a slight exaggeration of what goes on every day in many houses throughout the country. What housekeepers should strive at is to get a nice little savoury dinner, and yet at the same time to be economical. We will now take a simple case to illustrate our point, and suppose that the larder contains the remains of a cold leg of mutton, which leg has been decently cooked, and did not the previous day appear as a ghastly sight after a few cuts, like one of those horrible pictures in the penny journal that disgraces some of our shop-windows.

We will suppose the time of year to be early summer. A good many young wives under these circumstances would simply order a cucumber—possibly a shilling each—and think that everything had been done that was necessary; or some, still worse, would order the cook to hash the remains of the mutton—and a nice hash they make of it, in another sense of the word; for who has not at times seen that dreadful dish of immense size, covered with often hard slices of mutton, the whole swimming in a quantity of thin broth—we cannot call it gravy—in which slices of onion vie with sodden sippets as to which shall look the least inviting? Now, when such a dish appears, probably the husband, accustomed formerly to his club or college dinner, or the mess, says nothing; but he feels—"I don't mean to reproach you, my dear, but this is not comfortable."

Now, as the cookery-books say, suppose we give "another method." The cook in the morning early has cut off all the meat from the leg-of-mutton bone, and put it by in the larder. She has then chopped up the bone into small pieces, and put it on the fire to make stock, with the usual etcetera—viz., some onion, carrot, turnip, celery, and parsley. We will also suppose the house to contain some frying-fat, bacon or ham, and eggs.

The first dish we would recommend would be some rissoles. Take three or four small slices of the mutton, picking out those containing most fat, and one slice of bacon containing twice the quantity of fat to lean; chop up finely a small piece of onion rather larger than the top of the thumb down to the first joint, sufficient parsley when chopped fine to fill a teaspoon, about enough thyme to cover a sixpence, or rather less if the thyme be strong; add a little cayenne pepper and salt. Chop the whole ingredients *very* fine, or, still better, send them through a sausage-machine. When thoroughly chopped, the whole mass ought to be sufficiently moist to be capable of being rolled up into balls. If this is not the case, it only shows that there has not been sufficient fat put with it. These balls should be about the size of a large walnut. Dip each ball into some well beaten-up egg, and afterwards into some fine bread-crumbs. Fry them in some boiling fat for two or three minutes, which will generally be found sufficient to make them of a nice golden-colour. Next, for the gravy, which ought to surround them, take about half a cup of stock, add to it a little brown thickening—*i.e.*, some flour fried a light golden-colour in an equal quantity of butter—some of which thickening ought always to be kept in the house, as it will keep good for many months. Enough of this brown thickening should be boiled in the half tea-cup of stock to make it a good colour, and a little thick. Add a tea-spoonful of sherry to give it a nice flavour, and, if liked, a tea-spoonful of mushroom ketchup. Pour the gravy round the rissoles, which will be found none the worse for being warmed up in the oven. A little piece of fresh green parsley may be placed on each rissole, by way of garnish.

And now for the next dish, which will consist of mince with poached eggs. We would, however, remind the reader that the previous dish required bread-crumbs and boiling fat. In order to make the bread-crumbs, cut a large slice of bread of equal thickness, and having removed the crust, with a tin cutter or a small knife cut four pieces of bread the shape of a heart, about the size of a queen's-cake, and about an inch thick. Put these four pieces by carefully, so as not to break them, and make the bread-crumbs out of the remainder of the pieces, bearing in mind that the crusts will make an excellent bread pudding some other time. Then, when the fat is boiling for the rissoles, throw these pieces of heart-shaped bread into it. In a very short time they will become a bright golden-colour, when they should be taken out and placed on a cloth in front of the fire. Should there be any black specks on them, they will easily scrape off. These fried pieces of bread look like rusks in appearance, and their shape renders them infinitely superior to sippets as a garnish. Next take sufficient mutton for the mince, and chop it up, warming it in a small stew-pan with just sufficient stock to moisten it, taking great care it does not boil, as in that case the mince would be tough. With regard to giving a little extra flavour to the mince, besides, of course, a little pepper and salt, that is a matter of taste. Rubbing the bottom of the stew-pan with a bead of garlic is an excellent method, though of course it must not be adopted where the flavour of garlic is not liked. A small quantity of Worcester sauce may be added; but the general mistake is to put too much rather than too little. Next poach some eggs, allowing one egg to each person; pile up the mince neatly in a dish, and put the eggs on the top, cutting them neatly round, so that the yolk is surrounded with a rim of the white. Garnish the dish with the four fried hearts of bread, with a very small piece of parsley stuck in each, and have a little finely-chopped parsley—enough to cover a threepenny-piece would be ample—to sprinkle bit by bit on the eggs, which renders the dish prettier. A very little pinch of pepper may be placed in the centre of each egg. Care must be taken that the cover, as well as the dish, is made thoroughly hot, and of course the eggs must not be poached until a minute or so before they are wanted.

Two dishes such as we have described, served nice and hot, in rather small dishes than otherwise—how different are they to the large cold joint, or the immense dish of hash too often seen! Young housekeepers should always bear in mind that very much more depends on appearances than they think for. When alone—*i.e.*, tête-à-tête with their husbands —let the dining-table be made as small as possible, let the cloth and dinner-napkins be white as snow, and the latter exactly folded into some pretty shape. If possible, let there be a few flowers in the centre of the table. See that the wine-glasses are without a blemish. A smeary glass always betrays a slovenly servant, and the latter equally betrays a slovenly mistress. There is also no objection to having a green glass put to each person, even if no hock or similar wine be drunk; it brightens up the table, and looks—well, more club-like. If these little things—small in themselves, but they all tell—be attended to, a bright face and a bright pair of eyes will more than compensate for all the rest.

There are many good housekeepers who may read this who will say, "Why, all this is exceedingly simple, and only what everybody knew before!" Such, however, is not the case. The amount of absolute ignorance of the very first principles of cooking is far more common than many persons imagine. Again, too, with regard to the ornamental part of cooking—*i.e.*, the art of making dishes look nice and tempting—there are hundreds of fairly good plain cooks, as they are called, who seem quite incapable of grasping the simplest idea of the subject.

It is in this matter of taste, often, that the mistress will find her influence most beneficial, as her superior education will, as a rule, enable her to grasp ideas far more quickly than the uncultivated mind of the domestic. For instance, we most of us know the difference between a cold roast pheasant, perfectly plain, placed on a dish, and the same bird glazed and decorated with bright green parsley and cut lemon, and some of its feathers stuck in it in an artistic manner; yet there are, especially among ignorant countrywomen, many who would fail to see much difference. It is in this respect that the French are so far superior as a nation to the English, though probably the *highest* class English cooks are better than the best French. Compare, for instance, a French pastrycook's window in Paris, and one of a similar class in London.

In the above directions, recollect that there was some stock made. Now this stock, if it was required, would make a little soup in a few minutes; the addition of a little extract of meat, and a good pinch of vermicelli, being all that would be required. Suppose therefore your husband had committed that dreadfully thoughtless act, bringing home a friend unexpectedly to dinner—you would really have nothing to be ashamed of. The dinner would consist of some vermicelli soup, a dish of rissoles, a dish of mince and poached eggs, ornamented as we have described, and by simply ordering a savoury omelette to follow—very few men care about sweets—you would probably be rewarded after the guest's departure with an inquiry as to where you got all those things for dinner from.

On the other hand, think of the cold leg of mutton —such an inartistic thing when it has been cut into— or the dreadful dish of hash, which, somehow or other, has got as bad a name as a cold shoulder, although *properly*-made hash is a very nice dish.

How much better all this is than the ordinary course of proceedings—viz., the arrival of a telegram in the afternoon as follows :—

"Mr. A. B. to Mrs. A. B.—I shall bring home a friend to dinner—make dinner 6.30."

Mrs. A. B. instantly issues forth—the extravagance of the shilling telegram has its unconscious effect. She probably orders a pheasant, or any bird in season; some gravy-beef to make gravy; perhaps, in addition, a mould of jelly from the pastrycook's, which is not cut after dinner at all.

Ah! Mrs. A. B., a little more pains taken to make things look nice as well as taste nice when alone, and a little less ostentation and extravagance when you receive visitors, would make your home more happy. Your husband should never feel that he is the only one in the world for whom anything is good enough.

But if young ladies are ignorant of the first principles of cooking, what shall we say about some of the men?

I recollect at Cambridge, once, efforts made by two novices to make a sweet omelette. They thought that by breaking eggs into a saucepan, and adding sugar and jam, the result would be an omelette. With the slight *contretemps* of one or two of the eggs falling outside the saucepan, instead of in, and landing all shaking—perhaps with laughing—among the ashes of the grate, they got the ingredients in at last, and stirred them over the fire. After repeated failures—as, of course, without any butter it burnt almost immediately—they gave up their attempts, after exhausting their supply of eggs—sixteen in number—and wasting a whole pot of jam. One of these novices is a great friend of mine, and on one occasion when in Scotland he was one of a party who, during the season when all the hotels and lodgings were full, were obliged to take refuge in a furnished house, where, however, there were no servants at all. The party, all of whom were young, were quite delighted at the idea of managing for themselves for a few days. Everybody did something, and though it was some years ago, I fortunately had sufficient knowledge of the culinary art to keep us from raw meat or starvation.

A small cod-fish captured by one of us was brought home for dinner. The ignoramus in question was caught endeavouring to clean the fish, which he had got tightly grasped by the throat with his left hand, by pushing his thumb and finger down its mouth, and pulling out whatever he could from inside. And yet this man was an M.A. Cantab. It has, of course, been a standing joke ever since.

Now, when we come to consider how ignorant even educated people are with regard to cooking, what are we to expect when we turn to the poor? Too often persons will be found to exclaim against the waste, the ignorance, the extravagance, &c., of the lower orders, who forget that the fault to a great extent lies with the upper. In how many national schools in England are the rudiments of cooking taught, or even hinted at? The girl who in after-life will have to scrub floors, wash her husband's clothes, and cook his dinner, is taught history, geography, &c.; but surely it is equally important to her to know how to make an Irish stew, as to be able to name the principal Irish rivers. It is more useful to know how *not* to spoil shirts in the Wash, than to know King John lost his baggage there.

I do not for one moment mean to say that poor children should not be taught history, geography, and drawing, but that the first principles of cooking form a more important branch of education for them.

It is a common thing to find in the country that the only method of cooking a piece of meat is to stick a fork in it and toast it before the fire, letting all the fat and gravy drop into the ashes and waste. Of course, the difficulty to be contended with in any encounter with invincible ignorance is very great.

A clergyman once told me that years ago he had

the elder girls among the most ignorant of the poor instructed by his cook, in his own kitchen, how to make Irish stews and other economical dishes. They one and all succeeded in learning; all said that it was much nicer than what they got at home. Upon making inquiries, however, a few weeks after, among his parishioners, he found that in no single instance was the attempt made to introduce the new style into their own homes. Meat, when they had it, was toasted and wasted as before.

Were, however, every child in England to be daily taught at school the importance of economy in the preparation of food, the seeds of knowledge thus sown might sink into the mind, lie dormant for a time, but take root, and eventually bring forth a crop, the result of which would be to increase the wealth of the country, to how great an extent no one can say. The enormous resources of France are principally owing to the thrifty habits of the population. One of the largest employers of labourers in the North told me a short time back that a French workman could do double with his wages what an Englishman could. Perhaps the London School Board may some day consider the subject.

V.—HOW TO MAKE DISHES LOOK NICE.

I FEAR that as a nation taste is not our *forte*. I wonder, too, if there is any French expression that would fully convey the idea, " Wanted, a good plain cook." Wanted, a woman who can convert joints of raw meat into some state sufficiently intermediate between blueness and cinders as to render them eatable, and who also can make certain plain puddings, more or less heavy, as the case may be, but who has no more conception of artistic taste than a cabbage, and would be as incapable of making a dish look elegant as of singing the shadow dance from " Dinorah." And yet many of these persons are good honest souls, who mean well and do their best, but somehow or other it is not in them, and what is more, it never will be.

They have been born in an uncongenial clime. For instance, contrast the dress of an English workman's wife whose husband earns, say, £2 a week, with that of a Frenchwoman in a similar station of life, and yet probably the latter spends less in dress than the former.

We have already compared a French pastrycook's

window with an English one, but if there is ever a time in which we feel that Waterloo is indeed avenged, it is when we contrast a French salade with the ordinary English specimen.

It is somewhat strange, too, that the generality of cookery-books intended for household use signally fail to explain how to make dishes look nice. For instance, "garnish with beetroot and hard-boiled eggs," is a very poor direction to give to one of the above-mentioned good *plain* cooks. Some again give the lucid direction—"garnish prettily." Other works, too, are at times extremely tantalising to young housekeepers with plenty of natural good taste, yet without the faintest knowledge of the principles of cookery; they of course consult the cookery-book, which has perhaps been made attractive by some beautiful coloured engravings of dishes.

We can well imagine a young wife in deep consultation with her next sister a week before her first dinner-party, the cookery-book between them.

"Oh! what a pretty-looking dish," exclaims one; "let's have that."

Alas! the index is hunted over in vain, no description of how to make the dish appears at all; the next pretty-looking dish determined on shares a similar fate; and at last they give it up in despair, and either fix on dishes of which they have no idea what the appearance will be when done, or more probably leave it to the cook to do as she likes, with one or two little things from the pastrycook's—an expensive way of going to work, it should be borne in mind. I have been asked several times in strict confidence the question, "But ought it to have looked like that?" —a question often involving a necessary sacrifice of either truth or politeness.

Francatelli observes: "The palate is as capable and nearly as worthy of education as the eye and the ear." Now, without entering into the question as to whether a patty to eat is equal to a Patti to hear or see in the way of enjoyment, there is no doubt that the palate is to a great extent influenced by the eye. For instance, a large cold sirloin of beef on the sideboard at a good old-fashioned hotel, neatly decorated with bright green parsley and snow-white curly horse-radish; the dish resting on an equally snow-white cloth; its companions consisting of as tempting-looking a York ham, and some bright silver flagons, the latter enabling the looker-on almost to realise the "nut-brown ale" talked about of old, though what it was like we have not the least idea. There is a common saying, "It makes one hungry to look at it"; or "It makes one's mouth water." Yet contrast this same piece of cold beef with a joint I recollect being once brought up for supper at some lodgings, where Mary Ann was, to say the least, inartistic. She brought it up just as it was in the dish in which it had got cold—the dish smeary round the rim with Mary Ann's thumb-marks. The gravy had of course settled, and was thickly studded over with hard white wafers of fat. Some of the fat, too, had of course settled on the meat itself. Yet the meat was in every respect equal to the decorated joint, and many a poor hungry man would see no difference between the two, any more than a hungry bull-dog would. At least, some might even prefer the latter, in order to lap up the cold gravy with the blade of their knives.

A poached egg nicely done, the yellow yolk surrounded with an equal rim of clear white, in contradistinction to one badly done, in which the yolk has broken and run and got mixed up with the white, is another instance of how much depends upon appearances, for both eggs would be equally wholesome.

Now, there are few nicer and at the same time prettier-looking dishes than a salade mayonnaise. Yet too often when directions are given, in books or otherwise, how to make mayonnaise sauce, the latter point—that is, appearance—is altogether left out of the question. Making mayonnaise sauce, and simply mixing it up with some lettuce, and lobster, and hard-boiled egg, is certainly making a very nice lobster salade. Just in the same way the most beautiful clear jelly might be handed round in white pudding-basins, or even in the saucepan in which it was boiled; but how different to a handsome mould, with a few preserved fruits inside it, placed in the centre of a bright cut-glass dish, and a little cut lemon by way of garnish!

But we have been long enough on the subject, "How not to do it," and must begin at once.

First the ingredients:—A lobster; and if there is any coral in it, take it out, and make some lobster butter with it, as it will do no good to the salade. This lobster butter will keep, and enable you at a future period to make lobster sauce in a hurry out of a preserved tin of lobster; and this cannot be done without lobster butter. Next, some fresh lettuces (French are by far the best for mayonnaise salades), two fresh eggs—as we are only going to describe how to make enough for about four persons—some oil, and a little parsley. We will also suppose the house to contain some vinegar, a bottle of capers, a bottle of anchovies, and a bottle of olives, at the same time reminding timid housekeepers that these latter will do over and over again, and that probably a shilling bottle of each will last a twelvemonth.

We will now describe how a cook ought to proceed in order to make a good lobster salade.

The first thing she would do would be to put an egg in a saucepan, and boil it for twenty minutes or so, and then place it in cold water to get cold. Next, take a couple of anchovies out of the bottle, and put them on a plate (putting the bottle back in the cupboard; for if you get in the habit of putting each thing by in its place as you use them, you will never get into a muddle). Next, take a small penknife, and cut the anchovy open longways, and carefully remove the bone; if this is done properly, each anchovy will make four fillets or thin strips varying from two to three inches; wash them thoroughly in cold water, to remove all the salt and soft part. Dry them, and roll them up, as they look at times too much like worms if not rolled. Next, take a tea-spoonful of capers, and drain them carefully on a cloth, in order to thoroughly remove the vinegar in which they have been preserved. Next, take six olives, and stone them. This is done by cutting a strip off them as thick as you can, keeping the edge of the knife scraping the stone the whole time. As a rule, the olive will look round after the stone is taken out, but of course they have no ends to them. A little practice will enable the cook to cut out the stone quite bare, leaving the flesh, so to speak, of the olive in one piece, which curls up again, and looks like an olive that had never been touched.

These directions may to some seem unnecessarily

minute; but then we are writing for others who perhaps have never seen an olive except in a bottle in the grocer's window, and then they thought them preserved plums.

Next, chop up not too finely a little piece of bright-green parsley; enough to cover a threepenny-piece when chopped is quite sufficient.

Put all these things by on a clean dry plate for use —viz., the hard-boiled egg, cold, with the shell on; the anchovies, rolled up; the capers, dry; the olives, stoned; the parsley, chopped. And, as we have said, clear away what you have used before beginning anything fresh. Next, wipe, or quickly wash in cold water and wipe, the lettuces, and pile them up *lightly* in a silver or any oval-shaped dish. Next, remove all the meat from the lobster, not forgetting the soft part inside and the claws; cut it all up into small pieces not much bigger than dice, and spread the meat over the top of the lettuce in the dish, taking care as much as possible to make the shape high in the centre. A sort of oval pyramid may convey the idea, though it is not a very mathematical expression. Sprinkle a little pepper and salt over the lobster, and put the dish by in a cool place.

Next, the sauce itself. I believe the directions generally given to be wrong in this respect. It is a mistake to put in any pepper, salt, or vinegar at starting. I will therefore describe exactly how to make mayonnaise sauce, at the same time stating that out of the dozens of times I have tried, I only remember one failure, and that was on a fearfully hot day, and I had no ice.

Take a clean, cool basin, the size being one sufficient to hold about a quart. Next, take an egg, break the egg into a tea-cup, and carefully separate all the white from the yolk. This requires care, and the yolk must be passed from one half-shell to the other half very gently, in order to avoid breaking it. It is no use trying to do it at all with a stale egg. Place the yolk in a basin, and break it with a fork—a wooden salade-fork is best. Then drop some oil on, drop by drop at starting, and at the same time beat it up lightly but quickly with the fork. Do not, pray, get impatient, and put too much oil in at once. Continue slowly till the yolk of egg and oil begin to look like yellowish cream. When it once begins to get thick, you may slightly increase the dose of oil, or let the drops fall more quickly. Continue the process till the sauce assumes the appearance of railway grease. This is rather a nasty simile; but then it is so exactly like it, that it conveys a correct idea. You may now add a little white vinegar. Now, as the vinegar has the effect of making the sauce thinner—and the thicker the sauce is, the nicer it looks—this must be added with caution. A small bottle of dilute acetic acid, purchased from some good chemist, will be found best for the purpose, and is what I have always used myself, it being simply strong vinegar, about eight times stronger than ordinary; and, consequently, one-eighth of the quantity will answer the same purpose. Half a salt-spoonful will be found sufficient, and will not have the effect of thinning the sauce. Next, with a silver knife, or ivory paper-knife, spread the sauce over the lobster, till the whole dish, with the exception of where the green salade shows round the edge, has the appearance of a mould of solid custard.

Now to ornament it. First pick out about a dozen of the brightest-looking capers, and stick them lightly over the sauce. They will stick easily without being in the least pushed in. Next pick out about a dozen and a half pieces of the chopped parsley, each piece about the size of a pin's head, and drop these over it to give it a slight speckled appearance. Next take the beetroot, which of course is supposed to have been boiled and got cold, and cut it into small strips about an inch long, and as thick as a wooden lucifer match split into four, and with these strips form a trellis-work of beetroot round the edge of the salade where the sauce joins the lettuce, so that the bottom of each strip just touches the lettuce, but the strip itself rests on the sauce. The contrast between the red trellis and the white sauce has a very pretty effect. Next cut the egg into quarters lengthways, and place the pieces round the edge at equal distances, and put the olives and anchovies at equal distances between them; and also arrange the small claws of the lobster, bent at the joint, around the border. By this means nearly all of the green salade is hidden, and the effect of the dish is exceedingly pretty. The remainder of the chopped parsley and capers may also be placed round the edge, as when the dish is mixed up it will help to improve the flavour.

There is one thing more, however, that may make the dish look still prettier, and that is a little lobster-spawn. If the lobster contained any spawn, take a small piece and cut it up into little pieces the size of a pin's head, or a little bigger—a dozen and a half pieces will be sufficient—and sprinkle these over the sauce alternately with the little green pieces of parsley.

It has been described how to make a nice-looking little lobster salade mayonnaise for about four persons. When, however, a considerably larger dish, and several of them, are required, such as for a wedding breakfast or ball supper, you should get by way of garnish a few little crayfish or prawns. A small crayfish placed in the corner of each dish, with its claws outstretched, resting on the mayonnaise sauce, looks very pretty. If, too, the dish is of a considerable size, a small one may be lightly placed on the top as an ornament.

Now, we have described one way of ornamenting a lobster salade, but, of course, this is only one out of an infinite number of methods. Nor do we maintain that this is by any means the prettiest method; but we have given it as one of the simplest. For instance, mayonnaise sauce can be coloured red by mixing up some lobster butter with it, or green, by means of parsley-juice. Plovers' eggs, too, when they can be obtained, form a very pretty garnish. Leaves or flowers can be cut out of beetroot with a stamp, and be used by way of ornament. The long, thin tendons of the lobster can be arranged, too, to stick upright out of the centre, but they should be put in before the mayonnaise sauce is placed on the lobster.

Perhaps a few explanations of why the salade was prepared in the order named may not be out of place. It will be observed that the anchovies, capers, &c., were got ready early, but the beetroot was not cut up till long afterwards; the reason of this is, fresh-cut beetroot looks a bright red, but after some hours, if it gets stale, it has a sort of withered look, and turns a dirty reddish-brown colour; so too, with the egg: never cut open a hard-boiled egg until it is nearly time to use it, as the egg dries up, and the yellow yolk looks dark and separates from the white. The capers, too, were dried, as if dropped on to the spread-out sauce wet they would spoil its appearance.

Lastly, do not be disappointed if you do not succeed in getting the sauce thick the first time; and do not be afraid of the oil. One yolk of an egg will use up nearly a tea-cupful of oil. It requires a peculiar quick movement of the wrist, and, like whipping cream into a froth, it is not always learnt in a day. We fear that among the Mary Ann class, there are some heavy-fisted women who would never learn it at all. The dish, however, is well worth the trial, and if you can get one person to do the sauce and another to ornament the dish, all the better, as the exertion of making the sauce has often the effect of making the hand shake so much that it is incapable of arranging the beetroot, &c., with any degree of nicety.

VI.—BREAKFAST DISHES.

THERE are, perhaps, few meals that in this country vary more than breakfasts; and, indeed, it is not possible to draw any exact line between the hospitable and heavy Yorkshire breakfasts, including the huge game pie, and draughts of home-brewed strong ale at its finish, and the feeble breakfast consisting of thin dry toast and cup of tea, which with many is the limit of nourishment they can take early in the day.

There can, however, be no doubt that a good breakfast is very conducive to good health. There are, too, perhaps, few meals at which the appetite is more capricious than breakfast, and few occasions on which more depends upon appearances. A nicely-laid breakfast-table, with its snow-white cloth, crisp brown loaves, bright silver, neatly-patted butter, looking doubly tempting by contrast with the rich dark-green parsley with which it is ornamented; the juicy joint and tempting ham upon the sideboard; the rich, fragrant smell of the coffee—in itself sufficient to create an appetite.

But let us wait till the door opens, and the rattle of the silver covers is heard. First, say, a fowl done spread-eagle fashion, with mushrooms; next, some curried sausages; next, some mutton cutlets, with mixed hot pickles in the centre; while in another dish some poached eggs sleep peacefully on slices of rich juicy ham that have just left the gridiron. All these are placed on the table, while some grilled salmon, with which the breakfast begins, is handed round: many preferring hot muffins in lieu of bread as an accompaniment. But we must not forget the tankard, with the college arms emblazoned on its side, full of good buttery ale; for, as many probably have already guessed, it is a college breakfast we are describing; and Paterfamilias, when he shakes his head over the college bills, will do well to excuse a little of the extravagance of youth which breaks out in the form of breakfasts rather than suppers, the latter being conducive too often to the former consisting simply of a red herring and a brandy-and-soda.

With a dozen or more healthy young men seated round the table, free from the cares of life, indifferent to, and indeed ignorant even of, the meaning of the "money article," no wonder the tempting viands cooked by cunning hands rapidly disappear amid a merry conversation, in which the *summum bonum* of earthly happiness seems to be to row in the University Eight. But we must wait a few years. The bright-eyed youth with the fluffy whiskers, who performed such prodigies of valour in the last town and gown, has settled down into the sleek-looking country clergyman or lawyer; and his pretty, quiet little wife probably never dreams even of the life he led in the boisterous, but for all that really innocent, days of his college life. The college breakfasts and the college hall have, however, had their effect, and the change from the "college professor of cookery" (who probably is far better off than the tutor to Mary Ann) is—well, a change. The unvarying cold boiled bacon and hot boiled eggs will, in spite of the bright silver tea-pot, the butter-dish with the silver cow on the top, the lavish display of butter-knives (all wedding presents, of course), after a time pall upon the strongest appetite; but, unfortunately, if Mary Ann breaks down in one thing more than another, it is over the breakfast. There is an indescribable something in the appearance of the breakfast dishes she sends up that is not conducive to appetite. The yolks of egg have a tendency to run into the whites, and the fried bacon always seems as if it had been up the chimney, or under the grate, as well as in the frying-pan. An omelette is a hopeless impossibility, kidneys turn out tough, sausages come up burnt in one place and burst out like old boots in another, and when eaten, the bread-crumbs overpower the pork. After a series of failures, people settle down into the cold bacon and boiled eggs; what little change they do have consisting of potted meat, the most delicate palate being unable to distinguish between potted ham, potted beef, potted tongue, and potted game; for if there is one thing in the world of which the pieman's remark of "It's the flavouring as does it" holds true, it is of these shilling pots of potted meat.

That breakfasts will occasionally go wrong, is probably everybody's experience; to show how to make them always go right is not so easy. One great cause, in addition to ignorance of cooking, is late rising. Cooks sometimes start the day an hour behindhand, and never overtake the time. I am not sure that in judging a cook's character I would not take her as she appears in the morning coming down to light the kitchen fire. Some will be seen at this period fresh, clean, and bright-looking. This is a good sign, and augurs well. Others, however, come down yawning— no cap, the hair in an eccentric fashion, consisting apparently of one large knot at the back of the head. They have a fluffy and disagreeable look, suggestive of having slept in their clothes in a close room, the window of which has not been opened for months, and in which you would expect to find an inky fluid render itself visible in the wash-hand basin, were you to blow away the soapsuds. All this augurs ill for breakfast.

However, we will suppose the former of the two servants has come down, and that the dish for breakfast is the very common one of ham and eggs. First, the ham, which is probably in a slice or slices already. The first point to be considered is the state of the frying-pan; this latter should be perfectly clean before the ham is placed in it. Next, cook the ham rather slowly; with ham, poached eggs look better, and to my thinking taste better, than fried. Have a stew-pan ready full of water gently boiling, and drop in this water four or five drops of vinegar. Have a dish ready in the oven; and as soon as the ham is nearly done, take the eggs, which should have been carefully broken each one separately in a cup, and let them slide out slowly into the boiling water, doing two at a time; as soon as the eggs are in the water, place the ham on the hot dish, and so place it that an egg will stand on each slice. Next, take the strainer and lift each egg carefully out of the water, and have in your other hand a knife ready to trim off the loose pieces of white, so as to have the egg a compact mass, the yolk surrounded by an even rim of white. Next, should a little of the water rest in the bend of the strainer, mop it up with the end of a cloth before you slide the egg on to the ham, or otherwise, owing to the vinegar, the egg will taste acid. After the eggs are on the ham, see that all is placed uniformly in the middle of the dish, put two or three pieces of fresh parsley round, and send the dish up to table as quickly as possible.

In cooking eggs and bacon, fried eggs are best. Have, as before, the eggs ready in a cup, each in a separate cup. As soon as the bacon is cooked, place it on the dish, and put it in front of the fire. Then slide the eggs into the frying-pan with the boiling bacon-fat. Do this slowly and carefully, the chief point being not to break the yolks. It is a mistake to have too much fat, as that seems to increase those large bubbles that form themselves under the white. Take care, also, not to have the fire too fierce, or the egg will get burnt at the bottom. In taking out the eggs with the strainer use the left hand; and, if the white has spread itself too much round, or very unevenly, trim the white so as to have the yolk as much as possible in the centre. A knife will do for this purpose, but better still an old pair of easy-going scissors. Place these on the bacon, and look carefully over the dish, and wipe up with a cloth any appearance of "blacks" having mingled with the fat that has run off from the bacon, as this black grease, though perfectly wholesome, is disagreeable to the eye, and through the eye affects the palate.

We will next take another dish, cheap and nice—viz., bloaters. The objection to bloaters is the smell. If the cook has a private bloater for breakfast, the bloater himself informs you of the fact before you leave your bed. Now, bloaters cooked as they generally are—viz., whole—send forth a gust of extra flavour on being opened in the room. The best method of cooking them, therefore, is as follows:—First, shut the kitchen door; secondly, take off the heads, and split the bloaters open like a haddock. Have a perfectly clear fire, and having rubbed the gridiron with a piece of mutton-fat, place the bloater on it and grill it; four or five minutes will be ample time. When done, take a piece of butter, and after placing the bloater on a dish, with the skin-side downwards, rub the butter over the upper side of the bloater, and thus take off the dry appearance, and make it look moist. Bloaters cooked and sent to table this way are not nearly so disagreeable as in the ordinary way. Indeed, bloaters done this way often end up a bachelor's dinner-party at a club. Let us trust the claret is good.

The only way I know of getting good sausages for breakfast is making them at home. A sausage-machine soon repays itself, and is useful for many purposes besides making sausages, such as forcemeat, rissoles, &c.

The great advantage in making sausages at home is, first and principally, that you know what is in them; secondly, that you can flavour them to suit your taste. Some persons like sausages highly flavoured, some not. I will give you a recipe for sausages that I like myself, and would recommend you, if you like highly-seasoned sausages, to increase first the quantity of marjoram, secondly, the quantity of sage, and see which flavour you prefer. I would, however, warn you against increasing the quantity of lemon, as the result will probably be that you will taste the sausages not merely with your breakfast, but with your lunch and even your dinner, in a way better imagined than described.

The ingredients are as follows:—One pound of lean pork and half a pound of fat pork, or rather less; one tea-spoonful of salt, half a tea-spoonful of pepper, half a tea-spoonful of dried marjoram, one-third of a small nutmeg, the sixth part of the rind of a lemon, three good-sized sage-leaves. First, of course, take care that the pork is perfectly fresh; mince the lemon separately, as fine as possible, and mix it up with the other ingredients, having minced or powdered the sage-leaves. Cut up the pork into little pieces, and having mixed all up together in a basin, pass the whole through a sausage-machine, taking care to send the part that comes out first through the machine a second time. Roll the sausage-meat into small balls— the quantity I have named would make quite sixteen —and fry these balls in a frying-pan, and send them to table on little square pieces of toast. The toast can be dipped in the fat that runs out of the sausage-meat into the frying-pan.

Kidneys make a nice breakfast dish, especially when sent to table in company with a little fried bacon. The general fault is that they are overcooked, and consequently hard, tasteless, and indigestible. Some persons like kidneys absolutely blue inside when they are cut. This is, perhaps, going a little too far; they should, however, always be cooked so that when placed on the dish some red gravy runs out. A good-sized kidney is best cooked split open on the gridiron, and as soon as it is done, placed on its round sides, and a little piece of butter put on each half, on to which a pinch of chopped parsley is dropped. Sometimes kidneys are sent up skewered on a little silver arrow. A little pepper should always be sprinkled over kidneys while they are cooking.

The best form of having fish for breakfast is, undoubtedly, plain grilled. When those very small soles called dabs can be obtained, the best method of cooking them is simply to dry them, flour them, and then cook them over a clear fire on a gridiron—rubbed, of course, with a piece of fat to prevent the fish from sticking. Fish sent up this way should be put on an ornamental piece of white paper. The fish, also, should show the marks of the gridiron in light-brown streaks. A little pepper and salt should be sprinkled on them before sending to table, and a piece of cut lemon can also be sent up with the fish for those who like lemon.

There are very many dishes I could mention that are suitable for breakfast; but one word to those—and many such exist—who consider hot breakfast extravagant: the only dish of which they approve being eggs eaten with bread-and-butter. I would first remind them that the eggs and the butter in the shape of an omelette would be just the same, as far as expense goes; but I would protest against the custom of the day of young men eating, comparatively speaking, no breakfast, but taking a heavy meat meal in the middle of the day, about one or two o'clock, and then going back to work. A look into the City dining-rooms in the middle of the day shows to how great an extent this practice is carried, and also suggests how very unintellectual the greater part of City work must be. To really work with the brains immediately after an early dinner is, if not impossible, at any rate very injurious. Probably the seeds of chronic dyspepsia are sown by this unwise habit.

What men should do is to eat a good hearty breakfast; take a light lunch, say a few biscuits, or at the outside a piece of bread-and-cheese and a glass of ale, if this latter has not the effect of incapacitating them for work; and then to make a good dinner at six or seven o'clock, or later, as the case may be.

There is one thing in connection with breakfast that should not be omitted to be mentioned, and that is coffee. How it is that, as a rule, good coffee can no more be obtained in England than tea in France, is difficult to say. One great secret, however, of French coffee is that it is always not only fresh ground, but fresh-*roasted*. I would therefore briefly advise you, in reference to coffee, first to buy it in the nibs, and grind it yourself; secondly, never to grind it till just before you want it; thirdly, before grinding it heat the coffee in the oven for a few minutes—this latter having the effect of bringing out the flavour; lastly, do not grudge the coffee.

VII.—HOW TO GIVE A NICE LITTLE DINNER.

However strange may appear the statement, yet we have no hesitation in saying that one of the greatest steps ever made in economy in giving dinner-parties was the introduction into this country of the dinner *à la Russe.* It will be our endeavour in the present article both to prove and illustrate this point by contrasting a small dinner-party of thirty or forty years ago with a modern one. As we have already remarked, our observations are intended to apply to those whose status in society may be best described as possessing neither poverty nor riches. We will suppose the number of persons at dinner to be about ten or a dozen.

My mind now goes back to some people I knew very well in my younger days, and who will make admirable representatives of a very large portion of the backbone of English society: exceedingly kind, generous, and hospitable, but whose ideas of cooking contained a strong element of contempt for what they called—recollect, I am speaking of thirty years ago—French messes.

The time is soon after Christmas, and the party a

family one. The boys of the party, in their large white collars outside their jackets, look flushed and happy, and may be seen furtively looking from time to time at a bright yellow coin, which they keep in their waistcoat pockets—the coin in question being a recent "tip" in the shape of a Christmas-box from the stout and hospitable host.

But dinner is announced, and we soon find ourselves seated round a large table that may almost be said literally to groan with the weight of the good things placed on it.

First, some good mock-turtle soup—no doubt about it being a jelly when cold—a sort of soup that, in the present day of beards and moustachios, would require some care in taking.

Next the cover is taken off a huge cod-fish, big enough to have swallowed Jonah himself when he was a little boy, handed round with which was some oyster sauce as it should be, containing oysters in numbers. Ah! the very memory of it makes us heave a deep sigh. Good oysters could then be obtained at fourpence a dozen, and now—three shillings a dozen.

The present Chancellor of the Exchequer might well bring in a poll-tax on the men who eat oysters.

Next the four entrées were uncovered, and the silver lids taken out of the room, for the handles to be unscrewed, the dishes wiped, rubbed with a leather for a minute, and then they made four new silver dishes for the sweets. The entrées were as follows:— Oyster patties, curried rabbit, stewed kidneys, and what used to be called a beef olive—which consisted of a steak rolled with veal stuffing, and some very thick brown gravy poured over it.

After all these had been partially consumed, the covers were taken off what is termed the *pièce de résistance*, which consisted of a huge sirloin of beef, looking somewhat like the host himself, fat and jolly, with scraped horse-radish instead of grey hair; or perhaps a fine haunch of mutton, with a paper frill round its wrist, something like a lady's cuff.

At the other end of the table were generally two large capons, with a boiled tongue between them; beside which, two side-dishes, the one a pigeon pie, and the other a small York ham.

We will not go on to describe the second course. As a rule, lady housekeepers have no difficulty in superintending this part of the dinner. There are hundreds and thousands of ladies who can make a splendid dish of trifle or a mould of jelly, who would not have the slightest idea of gravy. It was but yesterday I was dining out where the gravy was handed round, which looked and tasted like pale, weak beef-tea, which in truth it was.

At other places, too, cooks seem to think that

when gravy is required, all they have to do is to put a little of the soup in the sauce-tureen, and send it up.

We would inform them that soup and gravy are two distinct things. Perhaps at some future period we may have a whole article on gravy, for gravy is a very weak point with inexperienced cooks.

But to return to the dinner above-mentioned. We do not for one moment wish it to be understood that we complain of it. It is a sort of dinner that makes people, when they come home late in the evening, at any rate feel they have dined, and do not, as is too often the case after some of those large dinners where fruit, flowers, and ice abound, on their arrival want a sandwich and glass of sherry or brandy and soda before going to bed. What we do maintain is that it is exceedingly expensive, and that a handsome little dinner *à la Russe* can be served up for less than half the money.

One strange thing in connection with the subject is that when the *à la Russe* style was first introduced into this country, nearly all those persons who may be described generally as homely people, who make a point of always keeping well in the wake of fashion rather than the van, we say those persons had an idea that the new style was very elegant, but that they could not afford it. We believe that there is still an impression abroad that a dinner *à la Russe* must necessarily be a very expensive affair; we will therefore proceed to describe a cheap but nice-looking little dinner, and, if space permit, how to make the dishes.

In the first place, flowers, like Mrs. Scratchit's ribbons, make a great show for sixpence. Where there is a good garden, there ought to be no difficulty in making a dinner-table look nice. All that is required is a little taste. It is well to bear in mind, however, that in selecting flowers dark-green leaves and the colour blue or violet should not be forgotten. We will suppose, therefore, the table arranged: the dessert and plenty of flowers, and nothing else, for we do not believe in the modern compromise so often seen —*i.e.*, some dishes placed on the table, as well as the dessert.

Now for the dinner. First—say the time of the year be the present—Julienne soup, bright as sherry, with just a taste of tarragon in it; a turbot or brill, with lobster sauce; a dish of chicken cutlets, white as snow, with little small green and red leaves in the centre of each, about half an inch long, and a little red lobster-claw representing the bone, served in a silver dish, with aspic jelly piled up in the centre. Another entrée of eggs and spinach—always a pretty-looking dish—some lobster cutlets, and some rissoles. Next a haunch of mutton—*i.e.*, a small roast leg of mutton cut outside the room haunch-fashion, parallel with the bone—and red-currant jelly handed with it.

In small households, where a large quantity of cold meat is undesirable, this is far preferable to a large haunch, and of course it is exactly the same thing, so far as taste and appearance are concerned, when cut. Next, by way of game, have some roast larks, served up in little paper cups containing a rich forcemeat.

Only one fowl, and that a moderate-sized one, will be necessary to make both the chicken cutlets and the rissoles. We will now calculate roughly the saving in this dinner when compared with the old-fashioned one we have mentioned.

In the first place, Julienne soup can be made far cheaper than mock-turtle; but we will leave the question of the cost of the soup out altogether. Next the fish; here again the saving only consists in the fact that it is possible to have a small fish when it is not put on the table, but impossible to have only just enough when it is. Now, warmed-up fish is never nice, yet how often do we see a splendid turbot or cod-fish go down, not a quarter of it eaten!

A cod-fish, by-the-by, is not a particularly easy dish for a cook to serve properly done and yet looking really nice. I shall never forget the look of dismay on a certain face when the cover was taken off a remarkably fine cod that had been specially sent down from a famous City fishmonger. The cook, too, was really a good one, and knew that raw cod-fish is simply uneatable. Probably the man, in bringing up the fish, had shaken the dish somewhat roughly, or set it down on the table with too much of a bang. However, the whole of the meat had fallen from the bones in a sort of shower on to the dish, and the gaunt skeleton remained alone, an awful sight, like some of those pictures of the desert with the remains of a camel being hovered over by one or two vultures. In fact, it looked so exceedingly ridiculous that nearly every one laughed, in which laughter the host wisely joined. It was indeed a pretty kettle of fish !

It is, however, in the entrées and joints where the great saving will be found. First let us roughly guess the cost of the old dinner: Sirloin of beef, or haunch, about 14 lb., 14s., taking of course present prices ; two capons, 10s. ; tongue, 6s. 6d. ; small ham, 12s. ; pigeon pie, say 3s. 6d., which would be cheap ; oyster patties, eight at 6d. each, 4s. ; beef olive, 2 lb. of steak, &c., 2s. 6d. ; curried rabbit, the rabbit being 1s. 6d., 2s. ; stewed kidneys, say 1s. 6d. Now this all added up comes to £2 16s. Next let us take the other dinner : One fowl, 3s. 6d. ; mushrooms, one tin, 9d. ; cream, 3d. ; lobster, 2s. ; eggs and spinach, 1s ; leg of mutton, 8 lb., 8s. ; calf's liver for forcemeat, 3d. ; larks, one dozen, 1s. 6d. ; about 1½ lb. of ham or bacon, 1s. 6d. ; which, added up, comes to 17s. 9d.

Of course it will be said that in the first dinner there was plenty left to keep the house for several days, and in the second but very little. This is perfectly true; but it is this of which I complain. The old-fashioned style was, when ten people came to dinner, to cook enough for thirty. This seems to me to be folly. Of course some allowance must be made for the character of the visitors; the little dinner *à la Russe* we have mentioned would be exceedingly unsuited to hungry schoolboys, or an agricultural labourers' feast; but then one doesn't ask these sorts of people to late dinners. The average guest is one who has had a substantial lunch—in the case of ladies—or one whose appetite is jaded with worry and anxiety, and requires a certain amount of tickling. The same dinner would not do for a dealer on the Stock Exchange, and a healthy country gentleman, who spends half his time on horseback, and has not a care in the world. We mention this, as one of the arts of giving dinners is to adapt the dinner to the guests, and the guests to one another.

But we must now turn to the practical part, which is, how to make the chicken cutlets, &c. First, early on the morning previous to the dinner, boil the fowl in some *clear* stock or some water; take it out and let it get cold; cut off all the meat, cutting the breast into thin slices; scrape all the bones, and place the latter back in the stock to boil down. If water has been used, the usual vegetables must be placed in—viz., an onion stuck with six cloves, a small head of celery, a turnip, carrot, a bunch of parsley, and pepper and salt. When the whole is reduced to about a quart, strain it carefully off; remove every particle of fat, and if not clear, clear it with the white of two eggs, by whipping them up with a little cold water, adding them to the stock, boiling briskly for a few minutes, and then running the whole through a jelly-bag. Next, again place the stock in an enamelled saucepan, and let it boil down to about a pint. Take a third of this and put it into a little enamelled stew-pan for the aspic jelly. Now, this jelly requires rather a decided flavour; add therefore a couple of beads of garlic, and let these simmer sufficiently long to give the stock—one-third of a pint—what may be called a foreign smell. The fowl-bones will probably have been sufficient to cause this to set into a firm jelly when poured out on to a plate and allowed to get cold; should, however, it not be firm enough, a little gelatine must be added to it. Should the jelly require a little colour, a small piece of toasted bread, such as is used for toast-and-water, will be found best for the purpose—of course put in when the jelly is hot. When the jelly is set, it must be cut up—two silver forks are best for the purpose—and piled up in the centre of the silver dish, for the chicken cutlets to be placed round it.

Next we have two-thirds of a pint of strong stock left in the saucepan. Add to this about half an ounce of gelatine and a couple of bay-leaves, and let it boil till the gelatine is quite dissolved; take out the bay-leaves, and pour it off into a basin, and take off any little scum that may have risen from the gelatine. Next pour some cream—about half a tumbler—into an enamelled saucepan; as soon as it begins to boil, pour the warm stock on it, take it off the fire, stir with a spoon for a few minutes, and pour it into a small basin for use. Now this white sauce, which is exceedingly nice, when cold will be a hard jelly, looking like blancmange.

Next take the slices of chicken and a few *thin* slices of ham, pour a little of the white sauce on to a plate, and before it has time to cool, cover the plate with very thin slices of chicken; dip the ham into the stock, and spread it over the chicken, again covering the ham with some more thin slices of chicken. Cover the whole, by means of a spoon, with some more white sauce, taking care to leave a little sauce for use afterwards.

Now when all this sets, which it will do very quickly, it becomes like a large white cake, barely half an inch thick. Cut this white cake into little oval pieces, the size and shape of the lobster cutlets, with a sharp penknife; take up each cutlet carefully, and with a small spoon, or end of a silver knife, cover the edges with the white sauce, which must be *nearly* set. Next cut some tiny green leaves out of some pickled gherkins, and some red leaves out of some beetroot, or the red skin of a chilli, and place four little leaves, two of each in the centre of each cutlet, star-shaped; a drop of white sauce will make it stick. Place a little piece of parsley, not much bigger than a pin's head, in the centre of the star; stick a little lobster-claw, three-quarters of an inch long, in each cutlet, and place them in a silver dish, round the aspic jelly, with a small piece of fresh, bright-green parsley between each cutlet, by way of garnish; and few prettier dishes can be handed round than the one in question.

The dish is somewhat troublesome, but then its appearance repays the trouble, besides which it does not require much standing over the fire. The latter part can be done sitting down. The basin containing the white sauce can be placed in a larger basin containing hot water, to prevent it setting too soon.

Instead of beetroot, a thin leaf of truffle looks much better, in which case a red bead of lobster-coral should be placed in the centre of the star, instead of the parsley. However, recommending truffle is rather useless, for the simple reason that persons rich enough to use them generally keep a cook, to whom these instructions would be unnecessary.

The next point is the rissoles. Take all the remains of the fowl—*i.e.*, about half—taking great care that no pieces of bone or skin remain, and chop it up with half the tin of mushrooms, and a good slice of fat ham. Chop up separately, *very* finely, a piece of onion about as big as the top of the finger down to the first joint; sufficient parsley, when chopped, to fill a tea-spoon; enough thyme to cover a sixpence; add a little cayenne pepper and salt. Mix the whole well together, and if a sausage-machine is in the house, of course run it through it; but if not, some pains and time must be spent over the chopping. Roll it up into small balls, dip them first into some well-beaten-up egg, and then into some fine bread-crumbs, and fry; and serve with some gravy poured round, exactly as the mutton cutlets were done in the previous article, though of course these rissoles are far superior to those made from mutton.

Next with regard to the forcemeat for the paper cases for the larks. These paper cases can be bought at the pastrycook's, but they are easily made at home, much cheaper, out of stiff note-paper. Take a quarter of a pound of calf's liver, cut it up into small pieces, and fry in about the same quantity of rather fat ham.

Chop up finely a bead of garlic, a piece of lemon-peel the size of the first finger-nail, a tea-spoonful of parsley, and the remaining half of the tin of mushrooms; add a little cayenne pepper and some salt, and enough aromatic mixed herbs to cover a sixpence (these herbs are composed of white peppercorns, cloves, one portion; marjoram, basil, thyme, nutmeg, mace, half a portion; dried bay-leaves, a quarter of a portion; well pounded and sifted, and put by in a stoppered bottle for use). Chop the whole very finely, and put it by in a small stew-pan to keep hot till wanted. Place a dessert-spoonful of this rich forcemeat at the bottom of each paper case. The paper cases should have the chill taken off them, by being placed before the fire for a minute. Then place a small roast lark on the top of each case.

Larks take only about ten minutes or a quarter of an hour to roast, according to their size, and ought to be eaten directly they are cooked. The cases should be placed in a silver dish, with parsley between them. This is a very savoury dish, and at the same time a very cheap substitute for game for a dozen people. Should there be no mixed herbs ready, a little nutmeg and mace will be found to flavour the forcemeat sufficiently for ordinary purposes.

Of course, in comparing the above two dinners, we have purposely taken rather extreme cases. What we would impress upon housekeepers is that many of these pretty, savoury little dishes, though they may give considerable trouble, are nevertheless very cheap. By simply looking ahead for a day or two, and a little industry on the part of others in the house than the cook only, a dinner often may be given combining elegance with strict economy.

VIII.—HOW TO GIVE A NICE LITTLE SUPPER.

The Christmas season is essentially one for parties— Christmas parties—those happy gatherings where old and young meet together for mutual enjoyment, and where the presence of children forms an excuse for grown-up people to enjoy a round game, or look on at feats of legerdemain with as much enjoyment as a middle-aged, grave-faced Frenchman feels when going slowly round on horseback on a roundabout. Perhaps if we were all of us at times more childlike we should be none the worse for it, especially in this high-strung, tear-away age. But I must leave off moralising, or else you, like the children at the party, will be thinking what a long time they are about the supper, which, after all, is the event of the evening.

As we have said, the party is a mixed one, and therefore we must manage our supper on the principle of meat for strong men, as well as milk for babes.

Judging by my own experience, there are few occasions on which I have felt more decidedly hungry than after a Christmas party. Really, to see some good-tempered persons hard at work amusing children, after perhaps having had a hurried early dinner, is quite enough to arouse pity. They have indeed earned their supper.

There are, perhaps, few opportunities for exercising taste better than a cold supper, where every dish is placed on the table at once. It would, however, be impossible to enter into the detail of the arrangements of the table without knowing with tolerable accuracy the resources of the establishment. For instance, where there are plenty of silver dishes, as well as cut-glass ones, to arrange a table handsomely would be far easier than where there are neither.

I would, however, give a few general directions. Have some flowers—real ones, if possible—and also mix plenty of green leaves with them. Try and alternate the dishes in colour. For instance, do not place a white mould of blancmange next to a dish of custard or a mayonnaise salad. Again, do not overcrowd the table.

We will go through a variety of dishes suitable for supper, explaining, where necessary, how they should be made, and also giving hints as to how they may be improved in appearance.

First, a very good dish is a cold roast turkey, glazed. What a difference, however, in appearance between one that has been glazed and one that has not! Did you ever notice a plank of mahogany just fresh planed, and contrast it with the well-polished flap of a Spanish mahogany dining-room table? Now there is almost as much difference between cold tongue, or turkey, or fowl, or pheasant unglazed and glazed, as there is between a mahogany plank unpolished and polished.

I will not enter here into an elaborate description of the proper method of making glaze, beyond describing it as good rich stock, boiled down till it has the appearance of strong liquid glue. In making glaze, great care should be taken so as not to allow it to remain too long on the fire. As soon as the stock begins to turn colour, remove the stock-pot from the fire, and quickly slacken the heat, otherwise the contents will get burnt, and much of the flavour destroyed, especially if the glaze be intended for the purpose of making either soup or gravy. The simplest method of obtaining glaze is to buy it ready-made—it is sold in skins—only take care to get it at a thoroughly respectable shop.

Now, to glaze a turkey is so very similar to varnishing one, that perhaps the easiest method of describing the operation is to say:—Melt some of the glaze in a little basin, and add, if you like, a very little water to it. Then take a fairly stiff brush and paint the turkey all over, drumsticks and all, making the breast particularly shiny. You will now see how very much the turkey has improved in appearance. It has, in fact, a rich mahogany look. If you are glazing, say, a couple of fowls, the principle is just the same. You will see the difference directly. By doing one first, and then comparing the two, you will understand the meaning of the simile I have given in reference to the mahogany.

Next, take some nice fresh bright-green double parsley, and fit some into all the hollow places you may observe about the turkey, of course trying as much as possible to make each side look alike. Place the turkey on a good-sized clean dish, and garnish it with some more parsley and cut lemon. I will try and describe, as some may not know how, the best method of cutting lemon for garnish. Cut a lemon in half the ordinary way, and then with a sharp knife cut off a thin slice, which is of course a complete circle, the centre being white, and the circumference a thin rim of yellow peel. Cut this in half again, thereby leaving you two semicircles. Next cut the semicicular rim— only the rim, or peel, or circumference, whichever you like to call it—through with a knife, and pull the two quarters of circles open with your fingers, till they stand exactly opposite each other. The hard white part of the lemon in the middle is quite sufficient to keep them together, if no violence is used. When I say pull them open, I mean only so far as, were another piece exactly like it placed over it crossways, they would again form a round slice of lemon.

Now, a lemon cut up in this way makes a very pretty garnish for various dishes, besides cold game and poultry—as, for instance, a boiled fish, such as a turbot, on which has been sprinkled some lobster-coral, surrounded with lemon cut in this manner, alternately with a little parsley and a few little crayfish, looks far different to what it would plain.

Just so with our turkey. There is one more thing to set it off, and that is, if possible, get a fine, small, white camellia, just tinged here and there with pink. Now, as camellias are not easily obtainable, and even if there be a few in the greenhouse, they would probably be coveted on such occasions as that we are speaking about for the purpose of adorning far more beautiful creatures than turkeys, your best plan will be to make a camellia.

How, you will ask, can this be done? Very simply. Cut it out of a turnip with a penknife. It really is not nearly so difficult as you would imagine. Take a sharp knife and a little scoop, and try and see how near you can get to making it resemble a flower. Then stick a little piece of wood into it, and tie on two or three bay-leaves. Take the feather-end of a quill pen, and dip it into the cochineal bottle, and just tint the edges only.

I have no doubt but that these directions will be followed by several young ladies with a taste for drawing. I should feel much obliged if they would write and tell if their first attempt was successful.

If you want to see these cut flowers in perfection, take a walk down Covent-Garden Market, where, if you choose to pay for it, you can receive lessons in artificial vegetable-flower making.

Next stick our flower, whether real or artificial, in the turkey; the shape of the bird and a little taste will tell you about where.

A tongue can be glazed in an exactly similar manner, a curly paper frill tied round the root, and a flower placed on it.

So, too, a ham can be glazed. But there is one method of ornamenting a ham which deserves notice.

We will suppose the ham ready glazed. Have you ever seen one, the top round the rim ornamented with a white substance which looks like beautiful white fresh butter, or even sugar?

Now, it is very easy to ornament a glazed ham with this composition, and one advantage is, you can put words on the ham, such as " A Merry Christmas," or, on the occasion of a child's birthday, the name of the hero of the feast.

The way to do it is as follows:—Get some nice white clarified lard, and melt it in a cup in the oven, and add a little salad oil to it, so as to make it thinner when it is cold.

Next roll up a sheet of fairly stiff note-paper like a cone, and hold this cone near the point in the right hand. Pour a little of the hot lard into the cone, and so regulate the pressure on the paper with the right-hand thumb and finger as to allow the melted lard to drop out or run out in a very thin stream at the point. This lard will settle directly it comes out, and turn quite white on getting perfectly cold. I would advise you to practise designs on a black shining tea-tray, as it will scrape off with a spoon and do again. With a little practice and a natural gift for such things—for a clumsy-fisted Mary Ann would make an awful mess of it—it is wonderful what beautiful designs can be formed this way, such as a harp or a rose.

In making a spiral border round the edge of the ham, it sometimes looks a little prettier to have a small pink spot in the centre of each circle. This is done by simply colouring the melted lard with a few drops of cochineal. But I would warn you against having too much pink in ornamenting. Just a touch, as in the case of the turnip-flower, is all very well, but it must be but a touch. We wish some persons would bear this in mind in using rouge.

Another exceedingly useful supper-dish is well-cut beef sandwiches. If these are cut thin, with just a little butter, mustard, and salt, you will always find them eaten. But a word about appearances. Have them piled up on a snow-white dinner-napkin, folded, if possible, at the bottom of a silver dish, and well garnished with small pieces of bright double parsley.

I need scarcely mention that every particle of crust must be cut off. Just contrast such a dish with what you get, say, at a railway-station refreshment-room the ham—they never have beef—coming out bodily with the first bite, and having a mouldy taste, which makes you regret that you didn't try either the butter-scotch or the Banbury cakes, which generally form the only alternatives.

Space will not here allow of my going through all the dishes advisable to have at a nice little supper, so I will confine myself to a few general directions.

Recollect you want to please children, without making them ill. Now, for the purpose I would always recommend a good large corn-flour pudding, made in a mould, and coloured a nice bright pink with cochineal. This can be made nice and sweet, and may be flavoured with a few drops of essence of almonds, or a little essence of vanilla. The dish is very simple and wholesome, and yet looks very pretty. You will very likely hear a little child say, "I will have some of that pink thing, please;" and, luckily, that pink thing is the least unwholesome thing on the whole table. It is the jams and pastries that do the harm.

With regard to jellies, I would add, try and get it bright. This requires patience and a jelly-bag. Also, as it will keep with ease, make it at least two days before you want it, so as not to drive yourself to have a lot to do on the day of the supper. In making jelly, whether orange or lemon, gelatine is the simplest, easiest, and cheapest method. Do not grudge the sherry, and also put a few coriander-seeds into the jelly when it is boiling. You will find this greatly improve the flavour.

But we must not forget the grown-up people, and under the circumstances they enjoy a good lobster salade mayonnaise. I have given directions before how to prepare this king of cold sauces. As, however, you are making a mayonnaise salad, it is almost as easy to make two as one. Have a lobster salad and a smoked-salmon salad. This smoked salmon must be cut into very thin slices, and simply placed round or mixed up in the salad just as it is—raw. If you possibly can, have these two mayonnaises placed in silver dishes, and get a few little crayfish or a few good prawns to add to the usual garnish of capers, anchovies, olives, cut hard-boiled eggs, &c., which I described in a preceding chapter.

In making mayonnaise sauce you will use two, or

perhaps three, raw yolks of eggs. Now what are you going to do with the whites? Why not whip them up into a stiff froth, and use that for ornamental purposes? For instance, suppose you have that nice simple dish, stewed pippins, on the table. Take a dessert-spoonful of foam shaped like an egg, and place it on the top of each pippin. Have also in readiness a few of those tiny, pretty little sweets called hundreds and thousands, and sprinkle a few lightly on the white egg-froth. Contrast this dish with the pippins as they were before. The change is marvellous, and yet costs almost nothing. Yet many persons would think, casting their eyes over the table, "Ah! that dish came from the pastrycook's."

One or even two piled-up dishes of almonds and raisins, being, if there are not too many almonds, dark dishes, form a favourable contrast with the light ones. A supper-table, to look really nice, must not have too many white dishes.

If you have a large centre-dish of trifle, with whipped cream on the top, a few hundreds and thousands sprinkled over it set it off. Now good whipped cream is rather beyond the powers of an ordinary cook, so if you happen to live near a really good pastrycook's, you will find it a good plan to have a man come round just before supper and supply the whipped cream, but make the rest of the trifle at home.

It is an exceedingly expensive dish to order, and, owing to wine, brandy, and liqueurs being requisite in its composition, one of the very last dishes desirable to order. Even pastrycooks will often spoil the ship for the sake of a ha'p'orth of tar, in respect of wine. To wit, mock-turtle soup. Order a glass of sherry at a pastrycook's with your mock-turtle, and throw half of it into the soup, and see what a difference it makes. In fact, as a rule, if you give a cook wine for cooking purposes, they drink the wine themselves, and manage the cooking without.

As a few last words of advice, in ornamenting your table, as well as in amusing the children, don't forget the crackers.

IX.—SPRING DISHES.

PERHAPS no season in the year is more eagerly welcomed than that of spring—earth's great annual resurrection from death unto life! How beautiful the first really spring morning! A warm, balmy air, a deep blue sky without a cloud, and bright sun lighting up like diamonds the water-drops on the fresh green grass, o'er which the feathery cobwebs drift for the first time in the year, the very spiders, in their wondrous instinct, preparing to set their houses in order, to welcome to their hearts the new-born fly.

The whole earth seems, like a huge chrysalis, to burst forth from its uniform-coloured shell, and vie with the butterfly's wings in beauty and variety of colour. Spring is, of all times of the year, the brightest, and the freshest, and the most beautiful!

"The rose is fairest when 'tis budding new."

Nor does the change of food come less acceptably than the change of scene. A moderate enjoyment of the good things of this world is perfectly justifiable, or our palates would never have been created; and while green hedges and fresh bright flowers delight the eye, a new set of dishes, rendered doubly welcome by a year's abstinence, delight the palate.

Who is there so lost to taste as not to appreciate the first dish of fresh green peas or new potatoes?—genuine healthy-grown ones, not forced, which latter are barely better than those preserved in tins. Then, again, the first piece of bright-red salmon, when it is well cooked; or the nicely-browned forequarter of lamb, with good wholesome English mint sauce with it—*i.e.* mint moistened in vinegar, and not a pint of vinegar to a small pinch of mint.

There is some very old riddle about spring being a lamb-on-table season. Whether lamb is really nicer than mutton is a question we will not now discuss; indeed, the question is entirely a matter of taste. There are, however, several little niceties in cooking lamb that inexperienced cooks and housekeepers should bear in mind. One very common fallacy is that lamb, being young and tender, does not require so much cooking as mutton. Such, however, is not the case. Well-cooked mutton, such as a haunch, should be cooked so as to be not exactly red, but very, very near it, and should hold what is called red gravy. Those who have seen a good haunch of mutton well carved will know how the gravy will settle in it after several slices have been taken out. I believe, at some regimental messes, many years ago, there used to be a fine for carving a haunch so that this gravy was allowed to run out.

Now, lamb should be cooked thoroughly, and should never even border on being red; underdone lamb is as bad as underdone veal. Of course, lamb bears the same relation to mutton as veal to beef. The climax of mismanagement is graphically expressed in the pathetic appeal of David Copperfield to his poor little "child-wife" when he said—"You know, my dear, I was made quite unwell the other day by being obliged to eat underdone veal in a hurry."

Another point to be remembered in connection with lamb is the gravy. A roast forequarter of lamb will not make the gravy that a sirlion of beef or haunch of mutton will.

Now, I daresay there are many persons who really do not know where the gravy comes from that usually surrounds a sirloin of beef; and as these articles are intended to instruct absolute novices, I will describe the process, reminding those who may think anything so simple unworthy of explanation, that even royalty some years back is reported to have puzzled over the intricate problem as to how the apples got into the dumpling.

We will suppose the beef to have been hanging on the spit the sufficient time, and the cook has arrived at the critical moment called dishing-up. Of course, under the meat to catch the fat, &c., that drops, have been placed that large tin vessel with a well in the centre, called the dripping-pan, which will be found to contain a pint, or a quart, according to the size of the joint, of melted fat, or, as it is usually called, dripping. The cook takes this dripping-pan, and carefully and slowly pours off all the fat into a basin; at the bottom of the fat will be found a sediment, brown or red; this is the gravy. Now, the great art is to pour off *all* the fat, and yet to avoid losing any of the gravy. What is requisite is—first, common-sense; secondly, a little experience and a steady hand.

As a rule, it is best to go on pouring till just a little sediment has run with the fat, and then stop. Next, take some *boiling* water, about half a pint or a little more, and pour it into the dripping-pan, and stir it about, taking care to scrape those parts where the gravy is dried on and the dripping-pan looks brown; by this means the gravy will not merely look darker, but will be absolutely richer. This must now be poured through a fine strainer over the meat. If the cook sees that the gravy has got a little cold in the operation, of course she would pour it, just as it is, into a saucepan and make it hot, but not let it boil, and then pour it through the strainer over the meat. When the party at dinner is large, and yet the joint put on the table, it is a very good plan to pour only half the gravy over at first, and to send up the rest hot about ten minutes afterwards, when it can be poured over in the dining-room.

Now, we have said that lamb does not make good gravy; when, therefore, it is possible, get some thin stock, and use that to pour into the dripping-pan instead of boiling water, only take care that the stock is tasteless—anything like rich gravy would destroy the delicate flavour of the lamb.

It should be borne in mind, too, that lamb is one of the few meats that are none the better for keeping; the quicker it is cooked, the nicer will it be. In hot weather, lamb has an unamiable property of getting high quicker than other meat, especially the shoulder. The reason of this is probably that it is "open," and not close meat, like a silverside of beef. A loin of mutton that has been jointed will get bad quicker than one not jointed.

We next come to the general and nicest accompaniment to roast lamb, and that is, nice fresh young green peas. When we say fresh, we mean lately gathered. Peas that have been picked some time are very inferior in flavour to those recently picked. Shell the peas, throwing them into cold water just like potatoes after being peeled. Next get a large saucepan of *boiling* water, into which has been placed a tablespoonful of salt, and a very little moist sugar—about a salt-spoon is sufficient. Strain the peas, throw them in the boiling water gradually, in order not to take the water off the boil for too long.

The next point to be considered is, why do some people always have peas looking a bright green, and others send them up with a bad colour? The secret of this is, do not cover up the saucepan. Now, as the saucepan is open, if the fire is likewise an open one, it follows that the fire should be pretty clear, or you will run the risk of having the peas smoky. It will, however, generally be found that the fire, after roasting a joint, is tolerably clear at the finish, especially as lamb requires a *brisk* fire. A few leaves of fresh mint should be boiled with the peas; they should be strained off very quickly, and put into a hot vegetable-dish, as they very soon get cold, and sent up to table very quickly. I recollect, years ago, that cooks used to put a penny (the old-fashioned copper ones) into the saucepan, the copper being supposed to improve the colour; but the use of copper for the purpose of making vegetables green should be avoided. In the case of bright-green pickles, where the colour has been obtained by this means, the result is that a very injurious if not absolutely poisonous compound has been obtained. Young peas do not require more than a quarter of an hour's boiling; old peas will take half an hour; and when old, a good-sized pinch of carbonate of soda may be put with advantage into the water, to render the water as well as the peas softer.

To say that mint sauce requires mint seems somewhat of a truism; but nevertheless this seems the point generally overlooked, especially at hotels, where the habit seems to be to send up mint in the very smallest possible quantity, and vinegar in exactly opposite proportions. Chop up enough fresh mint to half-fill a tea-cup, add about a table-spoonful of moist sugar, about three-parts of a tea-cupful of vinegar, and half a tea-cupful of water. Let the whole stand for a few hours, in order that the flavour of mint may get into the vinegar.

I don't know why, but servants invariably put too much vinegar; as nothing in the world will cure them, it is one of those things which, if it is possible, the mistress of the house should do herself.

New potatoes differ from old in this important respect: in cooking, the latter require cold water; the former, boiling water. In both cases salt must be put in the water, about a table-spoonful to every two quarts. Like peas, new potatoes are best when fresh from the garden. When really young, the skin will rub off with a cloth. They vary in the time they take to boil from a quarter of an hour to twenty-five minutes; but the best plan is to wait a reasonable time, and try one with a fork and see if it is tender, when they should be immediately strained off, as, if they are allowed to boil too long, they will get pappy. Let them dry in the saucepan, and when dry, put them into the vegetable-dish, with either a lump of butter—which will melt, and make them look oily—or a little good melted butter made with milk, into which has been put a little finely-chopped parsley, may be poured over each potato. Perhaps the piece of plain butter is best, however.

There are, especially in early spring, a large quantity of potatoes sold that pretend to be new, but are not. What they are, or where they come from (some say Holland), I don't know, but they are not worth eating, and it is just as well to know it. If anybody who understands the swindle will explain, I should feel much obliged.

To boil fish such as salmon is really very easy, but requires care. The fish must be placed in cold water, to which plenty of salt has been added—about six table-spoonfuls to every gallon of water, or nearly a pound of salt. Take care, also, that the water covers the fish, and that the latter is thoroughly clean. Rub the spine, which is apt to contain little clots of blood, with a lump of salt. Salmon always tastes best when boiled whole. When the water boils, take care to remove all the scum that will rise to the surface. As to the time it will take to boil, no time can be given, as this depends more upon the thickness of the fish than the mere weight in pounds. In carving a salmon, be sure to cut it always parallel to the spine, and not transversely.

The best sauce with salmon is undoubtedly lobster sauce, the best method of making which I have already described. I would remind you, however, again, that the sauce should look red, owing to the coral having been pounded with some butter and mixed in; also, all the shells and little claws should be broken up and boiled in the milk that will be used for the sauce, in order that the melted butter may be thoroughly impregnated with the flavour of the lobster. In making shrimp sauce, the same theory should be borne in mind. Boil the shrimps' heads, in order that the flavour of the shrimp may be extracted, only, before using this milk to make into melted butter, taste, and see that it is not too salt, as salt is often thrown over shrimps. The melted butter, into which a little lobster-coral should have been melted to make a nice colour, should then be poured on to the picked shrimps placed in the hot tureen; but shrimps had better not be boiled after being picked.

When salmon first comes in, it is best to have it boiled; but a very nice way of cooking salmon is to grill it—*i.e.*, do it on the gridiron just like a steak.

Of course, the salmon for this purpose must be cut in slices. Great care should be taken that the gridiron is perfectly clean. The slice of salmon can be placed on the gridiron just as it is, but if the fire is nice and clear it will be better to wrap each slice in oiled paper; by this means the flavour of the salmon is kept in. Of course, the cooking must be carefully watched, or the paper will very likely catch fire. The best sauce with grilled salmon is tartare sauce, which may briefly be described as follows :—First make some mayonnaise sauce as thick as butter in summer-time, add to it about a tea-spoonful of finely-chopped parsley, chopped on a chopping-board previously rubbed over with a shallot; mix this in with a good-sized tea-spoonful of French mustard flavoured with tarragon. The mayonnaise sauce is supposed to contain sufficient vinegar or *dilute* acetic acid. Grilled salmon is more suitable for three or four persons than for a large party, as few fires are capable of cooking more than two slices at a time, and one slice is only sufficient for two persons.

X.—SAVOURY SUMMER DISHES.

"It is almost too hot to eat." How often do we hear this remark during what is popularly known as the dog days! There is no doubt that as a nation we do not make sufficient allowance for the variations of our climate, and are too apt to feed ourselves and children on almost the same food both in summer and winter. The hotel waiter will give exactly the same answer both in July and December: "Dinner, sir—yes, sir—chops, sir—steak—cutlet," and he stops, having exhausted the English bill of fare.

But it is not so much in hotel life that the difficulty of getting suitable summer food is found as in home life. How many tens of thousands of men are there who from sheer necessity are compelled for the greater part of the summer to be cooped up in broiling weather in a hot, close office, their day's employment being varied but by occasional visits to hotter sale-rooms, &c., containing an atmosphere ten times more close and vitiated!

The unfortunate husband returns to his home with wearied brain and jaded appetite. Too often mingled carelessness and selfishness has provided such unappetising food for his dinner, that he is fain to seek for that nourishment of which his body stands in need in fluids rather than solids, and then the seeds are sown which eventually grow up and produce a harvest of wretchedness and misery.

I overheard a conversation once in a little back room in a famous pastrycook's, now done away with, between two wives, on their husbands' selfishness, each one of course trying to make out her own the worst. They had started with a basin of mock-turtle soup, and had followed with two oyster patties each. I left before they had finished. It was before wine was allowed to be sold by pastrycooks, or, judging from appearances, they would probably have remained there during the better part of the afternoon.

It is the way of the world all over. I recollect a man about five foot three passing one who was fully five foot two and a half, and remarking :—

"Dear me, what a terrible misfortune it must be to be so short!"

Do you know any one who breakfasts in bed every day, who never attends at all to household duties, and whose health requires a rarer wine at dinner than others? You may be quite sure that person will be most intolerant to any approach to self-indulgence in others, and will be given to hold forth little homilies on the duties of early rising, industry, and self-denial.

Charity begins at home, and those only who deny themselves can make allowances for the want of self-denial in others.

Great allowance should be made for those who, after a hard day's mental work, return home on a hot day, irritable, thirsty, exhausted, without being hungry. There is a great art in adapting the food for the occasion. There are a certain class of persons, especially in this country, who seem to fail to perceive that what is suitable at one season of the year is quite unsuited at another. For instance, hot pea-soup, followed by an Irish stew, on a broiling July day, is quite as much out of character as ices at Christmas-time.

In England, too, people do not seem to understand how to make the most of the means at their disposal for making themselves comfortable. How many thousands there are who, having good gardens, yet never use them except to walk in! For breakfast or tea what better spot can be chosen than a shady corner of the lawn; yet how often do we find this done?

Probably many would say, "Oh, but the people next door can see us." As a nation we are undoubtedly very shy and ungregarious. This latter quality, if one may be allowed to use the expression, is particularly shown at railway-stations. You may walk down a long train and find one man in each compartment, and each one glares at you if you attempt to enter.

The constitutional shyness of the middle classes has a strong ally in the constitutional rudeness of the lower.

Many years ago almost the only lunch obtainable in London was a Bath bun, washed down with tepid ginger-beer. But this bun had to be eaten under difficulties. First, the extraordinary height of the stool on which one was bound to sit made one giddy; then a crowd of small boys, with noses flattened white against the window outside, would carry on a running conversation, such as "Give us a bit, guv'nor," &c. Unfortunately, the faster you tried to eat the bun, the more it choked you; and as to the ginger-beer, it too often refused to go anywhere except to the nose. A lunch is still a great difficulty in certain parts of London. It would be an interesting Parliamentary return—first, the number of licensed victuallers in London; secondly, the number of licensed victuallers who sold victuals.

Were any one, some hot day, to place a small table on the pavement, and sit down and eat an ice, like thousands do in Paris, the result would be such a crowd that one would probably be locked up for the night, for obstructing the public thoroughfare.

There is, perhaps, no dish so suitable for hot

weather as curry. But there are curries and curries. I have seen some that have made me shudder to look at them. If you see pieces of meat on a large dish, almost swimming in a quantity of bright light-coloured yellow gravy, people will probably call it curry; but my advice is, don't eat any if you can get anything else. I will try and describe how it ought to be done. Say the dish is curried sweetbreads. The sweetbreads must be fried as directed in the article entitled "Uses and Abuses of a Frying-pan." The curry sauce must be poured round them directly they are done, and this sauce is made as follows:—

We will describe how to make enough for about six people.

First, take six large onions, and peel and slice them, and fry them a nice brown-colour in a stew-pan, using about two ounces of butter. Next take two apples, about the same size, or rather larger than the onions, and as sour as possible. Peel them, remove the core, slice, and add to the onions in the stewpan, then add a pint of good strong stock. Stir it all up, and let the whole boil till the apples are quite soft. Add to this a large brimming dessert-spoonful of Captain White's curry-*paste*, and a good-sized teaspoonful of ordinary curry-powder. The whole of this must be rubbed through a fine wire sieve, with a large wooden spoon. If you have not patience to rub it all through, you can't make curry.

The next point necessary is that this curry sauce should be made of the necessary thickness; and for the purpose, what I have alluded to before under the name of "brown thickening" is necessary.

Now, as brown thickening is almost an essential in every house where gravies and sauces are made properly, I will describe how this brown thickening ought to be made. As the process is somewhat troublesome, and a large quantity is as easy to make as a small, it will be found best to make sufficient to last some time, as brown thickening will keep good for months if made properly.

Take half a pound of flour, and, having thoroughly dried it on a large newspaper before the fire, sift it carefully. Next take half a pound of butter and melt it in an enamelled saucepan; a sort of white curdled substance will be generally found mixed with it, some of which can be skimmed off the top, and some will settle at the bottom. Skim the butter and pour off all that is as clear as good salad-oil, and only use this for the brown thickening.

Next mix thoroughly well together the sifted flour and the hot melted butter in an enamelled stew-pan, and stir it over a quick fire with a wooden spoon. If the flour has been properly dried, and the butter properly clarified, the whole mass will stick together, and shake about in the stew-pan. The stirring must be continued till the whole mass begins to turn colour. As soon as it is obtained a light fawn-colour, or looks like the outside of a nicely-baked French roll, remove the stew-pan from the fire, but still continue stirring. Throw in a large slice of onion; this will help to check the heat, and at the same time assist in giving the thickening a nice flavour.

It is wonderful how long an enamelled stew-pan will retain the heat. It would be a good lesson to an inexperienced cook to watch for how long a period the butter and flour will go on bubbling after the stew-pan has been taken off the fire. It depends of course on the thickness of the stew-pan, but this frying process will go on sometimes for ten minutes, or even longer, after it has been moved on to a cold slab. This fact will explain why hashes and stews are so often tough. Most cooks know hash ought not to boil, but how many place a stew-pan on the fire, and remove it on to the hob directly it begins what they call to simmer! They forget that the boiling, for that is what it really is, goes on perhaps for ten minutes after they have moved the stewpan from the fire, when a tea-spoonful of cold gravy, or even cold water, would have stopped the boiling at once.

Keep stirring the brown thickening till it ceases to

boil or bubble, and then remove as much as you can of the onion, and pour the whole into a stone jar—an empty white jam-pot is as good as anything—and allow it to get cold.

When it is cold it has the appearance somewhat of light-coloured chocolate, and a few spoonfuls of it will always give a nice rich brown look to gravies. It must be put in the gravy, and stirred over the fire in it; gradually, as the gravy boils, it becomes thicker. For ordinary gravy, when brown thickening is used, a tea-spoonful of sherry is a great improvement.

Cooks often thicken gravies, curries, &c., with butter and flour. The effect too often is that the gravy looks a light colour, and has a gruelly taste. A good cook should never be without some brown thickening in the house.

Sufficient of this brown thickening must be added to the curry sauce, which is supposed to have been rubbed through the wire-sieve, to make it as thick as gruel; and, as we have said, this thickening only takes place when it is boiled, and at the same time stirred, over the fire. The curry is now complete, and has only to be poured round, not over, the freshly-cooked sweetbreads.

Suppose, however, the dish required was curried mutton, which is, of course, a much more economical dish than curried sweetbreads, and it is undoubtedly one of the best methods of using up a cold joint. Cut some slices of meat off the cold joint; avoid skin and gristle, and choose those slices as much as possible containing most fat. Then boil up the curry sauce, ready thickened and finished, in a stew-pan, remove the stew-pan from the fire, and place the slices of meat in it, and cover them with the sauce; replace the stew-pan on the hob, but not on the fire, leave it in a warm place for half an hour, and just before turning it out make it a little hotter, if you like, by carefully holding the stew-pan over the fire; but recollect if it once boils or bubbles up the meat will get hard, and the curry will be spoilt.

The proper accompaniment to curry is boiled rice; this ought properly to be served in a separate dish. The rice must be boiled till quite tender, and then the grains should be separated from one another by being tossed lightly about on a cloth in front of the fire.

Curry is, as we have said, the most suitable dish for hot weather, as is abundantly proved by its being the most popular in India. In India fresh tamarinds and mangoes are, I believe, used instead of apples; various herbs and spices are also used, which differ in different parts of the country.

Many persons, especially old Indians, have recipes for curry. We have given what must necessarily form the basis of curry, where the curry-powder or paste is not home-made. By many, the addition of a little grated cocoa-nut to the curry is considered a great improvement; or where cocoa-nut cannot be obtained, a few grated Brazil nuts may be used instead. Others, too, strongly recommend the addition of powdered coriander-seeds. Coriander-seeds are, however, used in making curry-powder, and good curry-powder ought to contain sufficient. When, therefore, the powder is old, and has lost that aromatic smell which it ought to have, a little powdered coriander-seed may be added with advantage; but it has a very decided flavour, and must be used with caution.

One of the most common faults in inexperienced cooks is to have certain fancies for certain flavours, and then to let that flavour predominate.

I have tasted mock-turtle soup which might have been called marjoram soup. Herbs and spices must always be used carefully, and it is generally best to err on the side of too little than too much. To illustrate this point, I would mention what is generally known as veal stuffing. Who has not, at one time or other, tasted a turkey in which it was so highly flavoured that you tasted it all through dinner? Indeed, at times you may consider yourself fortunate if you don't taste it all through the next day.

How few cooks, too, understand how to use garlic

or aromatic flavouring herbs! It is in the proper blending of these strong flavours that one can detect the hand of the *artiste*.

There are many worse things to eat in hot weather than cold roast beef and salad. Now, it will often be said that if you want a good salad you must go to Paris. Certainly you *do* get a good salad there invariably; but it is equally easy to have one at home by simply doing what they do. One principal reason why English people so often have bad salads is that they have an absurd prejudice against oil. Very often, too, when they use oil, the oil is bad. Of course, it is as impossible to make a good salad with bad oil as it is to cook a good dinner with high meat. The oil must be clear, bright, and of a pale-yellow colour; if it looks at all green, it is probably bad. Bearing, therefore, this in mind, I will now tell you how to mix a salad, simply repeating the recipe or custom used in ninety-nine out of a hundred French restaurants. First get two or three small French cabbage-lettuces. Wash them, if necessary, in a little cold water, but do not dry them on a cloth, as you will thereby probably bruise them and spoil them. Shake them dry in a little wire basket; or put them in a cloth, and take the cloth by the four corners, and make the lettuce-leaves jump inside; then put them lightly into a salad-bowl. Next chop up enough parsley to cover a threepenny-piece, and also chop three fresh mint-leaves, and sprinkle this over the lettuce. Next take a table-spoon, and place in it about half a salt-spoonful of salt, and quarter of pepper; fill the table-spoon with oil. Mix up the pepper and salt with the oil, and pour it over the lettuce—I am supposing enough for about four persons—add half a table-spoonful more oil, and toss the lettuce lightly together for two or three minutes. Next add not quite half a table-spoonful of French white vinegar; mix it for a minute or two more, and it is finished.

Now the difficulty in many households is to overcome the prejudice against the oil. Perhaps some one, when they have read this, will do as follows: First take care to have a *fresh* bottle of *good* oil; then mix a salad as I have directed, without telling anybody how it is done. Let it be handed round at dinner-time, and wait and see what people say. If you tell them beforehand that there is nearly two table-spoonfuls of oil, they probably will make up their minds beforehand that it is nasty; but say nothing, and give the recipe a fair chance.

There are two additions to a salad which many think an advantage: one is to chop up with the parsley and mint one fresh tarragon-leaf; another is to rub a crust of bread with a piece of garlic, and then put the crust into the salad-bowl, and toss it about with the salad. This is quite sufficient to give it a decided flavour of garlic, and, where garlic is not disliked, will be found to be a decided improvement.

XI.—SALADS, AND HOW TO MAKE THEM.

THERE can be no doubt that the last ten or fifteen years have witnessed, if not a revolution, at any rate a very great change in the domestic habits of the middle classes of this country. Persons nowadays drink wine every day who twenty years back looked upon a glass of port after a Sunday's early dinner as a rare luxury. There are probably more cases of champagne consumed in a month now than bottles in a week of the time of which we speak. In many households we regret to see brandies-and-sodas have taken the place of good old-fashioned home-brewed ale. But in the general management of the table the universal increase in the undoubtedly luxurious habits of the age is still more marked. In every class of society dinners are served in the present day which would have simply astounded our forefathers. Now, were we to inquire into the cause of this change, our subject would be political rather than domestic economy. The freer intercourse, not merely amongst ourselves, but with our foreign neighbours, the alteration in the value of money, the great increase in the importation of foreign goods of various descriptions, have all had their effect. Again, it must be borne in mind that increased luxury in one sense does not necessarily mean increased expenditure. We have before had occasion to contrast the old-fashioned heavy English dinner with a modern one *à la Russe*, and have endeavoured to explain that the latter, while far more luxurious, is at the same time far more economical.

If there is any dish in the world that varies more than another, probably it is a salad, and at the same time it may be considered as one of the cheapest of modern luxuries, which by some is considered almost an essential to the every-day dinner. Contrast what we may call the early English style with the modern French. First, that huge lettuce, sliced up, saturated in a pint or two of vinegar; it never even reached the dignity of being eaten alone, but was considered a proper accompaniment to a strong cheese, the unavoidable noise made in masticating it unfortunately invariably drowning what little conversation there was. Second, the *salade à la Française* as one gets it in Paris: soft, delicious, digestible, and somehow or other containing some subtle flavour that seems at present to have baffled the research of the most intelligent foreigner with the astutest taste. Of course, too, tastes differ and require training. Many of the lower orders in this country, were they to see a

Frenchman in humble life dress a salad, using the oil as he does, would regard him with feelings somewhat akin to what the Frenchman would feel were he to witness the national feat of drinking off a quart of adulterated beer as an appetiser before breakfast. Each countryman would regard the other as a beast. But we must come to the practical part of our subject, and endeavour to improve upon the lettuce and vinegar, though by preface we would state that that by no means small class who think the best part of the salad *is* the vinegar, which they keep to the last, like a child with the jam part of a tart, and lap up finally with the assistance of a blade of a steel knife, will find but little instruction from our remarks.

We will commence with giving simple instructions for dressing an ordinary salad, composed of plain lettuce.

First, have ready a salad-bowl sufficiently large to enable the salad-dresser to toss the lettuce lightly together. Next, the lettuce should be crisp, but not too hard, and we would advise that hard stalk part (which, by the way, many persons think the best part) not to be put in. This, of course, however, is a matter of taste. Then, if possible, don't wash the lettuce at all; examine every leaf carefully and wipe it clean, and remove any specks of garden-mould that may be on it, and in wiping be particularly careful not to crush or bruise the lettuce. Sometimes, and indeed often, washing is absolutely indispensable; when this is the case, however, bear in mind the importance of leaving the lettuce to soak in the water as little as possible; next, when the lettuce has been washed, it must of course be dried; the best plan being to shake it in a little wire basket, which can be swung round in the open air. These wire baskets are sold in the streets by men who go about with skewers and penny gridirons, and are well worth buying. If you possess a whitebait-basket, that will answer the purpose admirably.

Another method of drying the lettuce is to put it in a clean, dry cloth, and take the cloth by the four corners and shake it lightly; the drops of water shake off, and are absorbed by the cloth, but the lettuce does not get bruised. Next chop up finely about enough parsley to fill a small salt-spoon, and with it one or two leaves of fresh tarragon (we will suppose you are mixing salad enough for four persons); sprinkle this over the lettuce in the bowl, which, if the flavour is liked, may be first rubbed inside with a slice of onion, or better still, a bead of garlic. In giving this onion or garlic flavour to a salad, too great care cannot be taken to avoid overdoing it. Sydney Smith wrote a recipe on dressing salad, so well known that we will not repeat it in full, with the exception of the two admirable lines which every one should know by heart :—

> "Let onion's atoms lurk within the bowl,
> And, scarce suspected, animate the whole."

There are various ingredients used in cooking which can only be used as here directed—viz., "scarce suspected." Garlic is essentially one of these, as well as nutmeg, allspice, mace, &c. But to return to the salad which requires dressing. Place in a table-spoon a small salt-spoonful of salt, about half of pepper, then fill up the spoon with good fresh Lucca oil, stir it quietly with a fork, and pour over the salad and toss it lightly about; add another table-spoonful of oil, and continue the mixing; and finish by adding about half a table-spoonful of English vinegar, or rather less of French white-wine vinegar. We ought in this country to be very careful before we set up our opinions on such a subject as cooking before the French. Now, some French cookery-books I have seen maintain that in dressing a salad it does not matter whether you put in the oil first or the vinegar. For my part I think it does. If the vinegar be put in *before* the oil, it is apt to be absorbed by the lettuce-leaves, and consequently one part of the salad will taste sharper than the other; while if the oil be put in first, and the salad well mixed, each leaf gets coated with oil, and the small quantity of vinegar when added is generally diffused. To my taste the king of salad-dressings is mayonnaise sauce, but before refreshing your memories as to how to make it, I will first describe two exceedingly nice salads, which have the advantage of using up cold vegetables. The first is asparagus salad, and as absolutely no oil is used in compounding it, a description may raise the hopes of some of my readers, who somehow "never will believe in oil." We will suppose some properly-boiled asparagus has been left from dinner. All that is necessary is to dip the eatable parts or tops in the following sauce. Place the asparagus on a dish, and if any remains over from the sauce pour it on the tops; the sauce being made as follows:—Melt, but do not heat too much, a little butter—say an ounce—and pour it on to a plate; mix in with a fork a good teaspoonful of made mustard, a little pepper and salt, and nearly a dessert-spoonful of English vinegar; stir it all up quickly, and dip in the ends of the asparagus as directed. This is a capital way of using up asparagus, and the salad makes an excellent dish at a supper confined to cold meats.

The other salad to which we refer is the old-fashioned dish, potato salad, and is the best made from new potatoes, or rather from potatoes not too old and floury. Considering the number of houses where potatoes are left from the early dinner, and where there is afterwards a supper, it seems strange that potato salad does not form a more frequent dish than it does. The way in which it is compounded is extremely simple. The "suspicion of onion"—which can be brought about as before, by simply rubbing the bowl, or if a rather strong flavour of onion is not objected to, by chopping up a small piece of onion finely and adding to the salad—is one requisite; then slice the potatoes, place them in the bowl, add a little chopped parsley, and if liked, as before, tarragon, and dress the salad exactly as the lettuce was directed to be dressed, adding a little more or less vinegar, according to taste.

We must not, in enumerating the various rarer kinds of salad, omit to mention the ordinary English salad and its dressing. The ordinary English salad is a mixture of lettuce, mustard and cress, beetroot, radishes; to which are sometimes added endive and celery. If in season, a little celery is certainly an improvement to a mixed salad of this kind; and some even recommend a few slices of boiled potatoes. The usual dressing to a salad of this description is made by mixing three or four table-spoonfuls of cream with half a table-spoonful or more of brown sugar, two table-spoonfuls of vinegar, about a tea-spoonful of made mustard, pepper and salt, and some add a little oil, though when cream is used there is no occasion for oil, and those who prefer this kind of salad generally object to it.

In dressing mixed salads the variety of recipes is almost innumerable. Yolks of hard-boiled eggs are mixed up with a little milk, and when cream is liked and yet cannot be obtained, this is a very good substitute. Of course, in winter the choice of salad is limited, though of late years it is possible to obtain French lettuces nearly all the year round. Still, a very nice salad can be made from mixed endive, beetroot, and celery, which can be dressed in any of the ways I have mentioned.

An exceedingly nice salad can be formed from mixed boiled vegetables, the most important ones being cauliflower, French beans, peas, summer cabbage, and new potatoes; a little chopped parsley and young onions should be added, and the salad dressed exactly similar to the potato salad.

A variety of herbs are used abroad for salads, which are not often used in this country, the chief being dandelion-leaves. These herbs, however, are difficult to obtain except in the neighbourhood of Soho, where a knowledge of French is requisite in addition, in order for you to obtain exactly what you want; and as there are herbs closely resembling those used, some of which are absolutely poisonous, caution should be used by amateur herbalists. The fact, however, remains that French peasants would gather a delicious salad from our ditches, whereas the only creature in the country sufficiently educated to appreciate these delicacies at present is the British pig.

By far the best form of sauce for salads is mayonnaise sauce, especially when the salads consist of some green vegetable, such as lettuce, mixed with meat or fish. For instance, we can have chicken salad, lobster salad, or salmon salad, &c. Now with salad of this description no sauce can approach, either in appearance or flavour, the mayonnaise sauce. As I have already given full instructions as to the best method of preparing this sauce, in the article entitled "How to Make Dishes Look Nice," I will briefly remind you that the one great secret in getting the sauce thick is to drop the oil on the yolk of egg very slowly, drop by drop at starting, and also not to put the vinegar in the basin with the yolk at the commencement, as is often erroneously taught. By dropping the oil one drop at a time, and by patiently beating up the yolk of egg, the sauce will gradually assume the form of custard, and by adding more oil, and continuing the beating, can be made as firm as butter. A little salt and white pepper and French white-wine vinegar can then be carefully added; but it will be often found best to defer adding the pepper, salt, and vinegar till the salad is all mixed up together. As mayonnaise is, when properly made a firm sauce, it is particularly useful in masking over salads, thereby rendering them very ornamental dishes. For instance, suppose you have a few slices of smoked salmon—and smoked salmon, lettuce (especially small French ones), and mayonnaise sauce make one of the nicest salads that can be got—the following is the best method of preparing a really ornamental dish:—Pile the lettuce up in the centre of the dish as high as possible, and so arrange it that the outer leaves are smooth and uniform; cover these leaves entirely with the sauce, using if possible a silver knife or ivory paper-knife for the purpose; place the slices of salmon neatly round the base of the salad, which ought in appearance to resemble a mould of solid custard. Ornament the sauce by dropping on little pieces of finely-chopped parsley, and sticking in a few dried capers, and stick a little sprig of bright-green parsley on the top; a few olives and anchovies are a great improvement. A dish of this description makes a very pretty addition either to the supper-table or at lunch. I need scarcely add that hard-boiled eggs cut up form a capital garnish to almost every kind of salad. The eggs, to taste nice, should be new-laid. They should be placed in a saucepan in *cold* water, and allowed to remain in a quarter of an hour or twenty minutes after the water boils; they should then be taken out and placed in cold water, and had better not be peeled and cut up till within, say, half an hour of the salad being eaten, as hard-boiled egg is apt to change its colour if exposed to the air too long. When a silver dish is used, the egg will discolour it very much, so bear in mind to clean it as soon as possible. Mayonnaise sauce will keep two or even more days, if kept in a very cool place.

XII.—PICNIC DAINTIES.

THERE are perhaps few months that test the cook's art more than that of August; and not only the cook, but the housekeeper, must exercise some little tact, in order to avoid the waste that too often ensues from heat and thunderstorms.

We live in so variable a climate that housekeepers are at times apt to forget that, though in winter a haunch of mutton will hang for a month, and be all the better for it, yet there are occasional days on which meat that has been killed in the early morning is bad by sunset.

It is these sultry days that seem to invite us to wander forth into some shady wood, and, stretched on the soft green turf, eat cooling food and imbibe cooling drinks, by the side of some clear rippling brook. Nor should we necessarily, whatever be the weather, enjoy our lunch the less for a little society — in other words, August hot days are admirably adapted for picnics.

Picnic! the very name conjures up before my eyes hundreds of faces. Wonderful institution! almost the only one that seems capable of driving that curse of English society, formality, out of the field.

First, the unpacking of the huge hampers, at times necessitating almost the diving in of two heads at once—bright eyes meet under cover of the unromantic wickerwork, and look brighter for the meeting. It is wonderful, by-the-by, how stooping over a hamper causes most people to flush. Ah! happy time; when most are young, and the world before them as fresh, as bright, and as green as the grass on which they sit. How many staid old married couples are there who can look back upon a picnic as the starting-point in their long road of happiness. No rose, however, without a thorn. How many, too, can look upon the same festive occasion, and remember as if yesterday the sharp sting of the green-eyed monster, then felt for the first time, and the poison of which has blighted a lifetime!

> "Lift not the festal mask, enough to know
> No scene of mortal life but teems with mortal woe."

Fortunately, we are not all moulded alike by the parent hand of Nature.

The majority, in fact, pass in early life from face to face like the butterfly from flower to flower, seeing no difference beyond that the present one is always the sweetest, and at last settle down into a humdrum life, as unacquainted with the heaven of love as they are incapable of feeling the stings of disappointment.

> "How much, methinks, I could despise this man,
> But that in charity I am bound against it."

But the very class of whom we are speaking—viz., the majority—have probably long ere this looked for the practical part of the subject to commence—viz., the lobster salad, pigeon pie, cucumber, ice, champagne, &c.

A few hints on the general management of picnics may possibly be of service.

All know the difference between one well-managed and one ill-managed. The things most generally forgotten are the knives and forks and the salt. The most awful thing of all to forget is the hamper containing the drinkables. One indispensable thing for the comfort of a picnic on a hot day is a large lump of ice. If this is well covered in sawdust, and wrapped round with a blanket or thick cloth, it is wonderful how little will melt even in a long journey.

We will run hastily through the ordinary picnic dishes, with a word or two to say on each.

First, cold lamb and mint sauce. Bear in mind that the former is very apt to turn quickly, in hot weather, especially if packed close, or put in a hamper near the top exposed to the sun. Pepper the joint, and wrap it up in cool cabbage-leaves. The mint sauce must be put in a small bottle, a stone ginger-beer bottle being as good as anything.

Second, lobster salad. This of course is dressed on the ground. Take care, however, in packing the lobsters, that they do not impart a fishy flavour to everything else. A few hard-boiled eggs should be taken to garnish the salad.

Pigeon pie. A good pigeon pie ought to have plenty of gravy, and this gravy when cold should be properly a firm jelly. I recollect once in a picnic the pigeon pie had leaked, and the gravy had soaked quite through the table-cloth, which had been placed folded up near it in the hamper. Now a very little trouble would have avoided this in making the gravy for the pie, bearing in mind the time of year, and how unlikely gravy is to set firm unless made exceedingly strong. All the cook has to do is to put in a little gelatine. This will insure the gravy being firm when cold.

A cucumber properly dressed is an exceedingly nice accompaniment to cold fowl and cold meat in hot weather, and perhaps never appears to better advantage than at a picnic. A cucumber improperly dressed is a very different thing, however. Who has not at times at hotels or restaurants met with the small glass dish containing thin slices of cucumber soaked in vinegar, on which float a few spots of oil, looking more like the fat on beef-tea before it is cold?

How utterly uneatable is the cucumber in question, simply because the waiter was too ignorant to know how to dress it! The cucumber must be sliced very thin, and of course all the green peel removed before slicing. These slices must next be placed in a dish with a good-sized pinch of salt, and then covered with fresh oil, and well mixed up; they may now be peppered and mixed again, the vinegar, in very small quantities, being added last of all. The cucumber, being well covered with oil to begin with, will not soak up the vinegar and taste like sour pickle.

I have already given directions how to make claret-cup. When claret-cup is required for a picnic, it will be found best to take ready mixed in a small bottle some plain syrup, and also in another bottle a little sherry, brandy, and noyeau, mixed in the proportions I named before. All, therefore, that is required is a strip of the peel from the cucumber and a slice of lemon to be added to a bottle of claret, the mixed wine and spirit out of the bottle next, a little syrup, a lump of ice, and a couple of bottles of soda-water to finish with.

An exceedingly delicious and at the same time un-intoxicating drink is some syrup of pineapple added to a bottle of soda-water and a lump of ice. This syrup can be obtained at S. Sainsbury's, 177, Strand—I mention the name, as I do not know of any other place where it can be obtained; and really in the present day anything that assists temperance deserves mention. Perhaps the most important element towards the success of a picnic is good temper and the absence of selfishness. Just as on board ship there seems a sort of mutual understanding that every one must be pleasant, so is there in these little happy gatherings. Of course, too, much depends on the selection of the company. Avoid asking those who invariably act as wet blankets on anything approaching to fun or merriment.

But, however hot the weather, we cannot have a picnic every day, though some may have thoughts on the subject similar to the little jockey-boy, who wished it was Derby-day all the year round. We must eat to live, which is better than simply living to eat.

Mushrooms *au gratin* form a very good dish for hot weather, but as fish is eaten first I should remind those who suffer from the heat, and consequent loss of appetite, that what is known as fish souchet is an admirable thing to start dinner with. Those who have dined at fish dinners at Greenwich, or, still better, Gravesend, as the latter is nearer the sea, will remember how exceedingly nice was the flounders souchet which generally constitutes the first course at those admirable little dining-places like the "Old Falcon," at Gravesend. The neat-looking thin slices of brown bread and butter somehow make one hungry to look at them, so suggestive of the *real* whitebait to follow. The preparation of flounders souchet is very simple. First boil the fish in some water with a little salt till they are tender. Then take off carefully all the scum, and lift the fish one by one into a vegetable-dish nearly full of boiling water, taking care in so doing not to break the fish. Throw in one or two sprigs of fresh green parsley, and the dish is complete. Hand round with the fish some thin slices of brown bread and butter. Eels souchet is very nice, and we described how to make it under the heading of turtle soup. When flounders cannot be obtained, those very small soles, sometimes called, I think, dabs, make a capital souchet; a large dish need not cost sixpence; but pray don't forget the brown bread and butter.

It is wonderful sometimes, by a little forethought, how a dinner can be improved. Out of the many hundreds who have enjoyed those fish souchets at fish dinners, I wonder to how many the idea ever occurred —"I must have this at home."

Mushrooms *au gratin* form a more elaborate dish. For this purpose only large cup-mushrooms should be used. Suppose, then, we have eight or ten fine cup-mushrooms—and by cup I mean the top of the mushroom round, and capable of being made hollow. First cut off all the stalks, and peel them, and also peel very carefully the cup-like part of the mushroom, so as not to hurt the rim. Next scoop out the inside of these cups, and chop it up with the stalks of the mushrooms. Take a piece of shallot about as big as the top of the thumb down to the first joint, and sufficient parsley when chopped fine to fill a tea-spoon, and sufficient thyme to cover a shilling. Chop all these up together very fine, adding a little cayenne pepper. Next take some raw bacon and scrape it. It will be found that the fat will scrape easily, but not the lean. This latter must occasionally be cut in strips. Continue scraping the bacon till you have got about three ounces altogether. Chop the lean as fine as possible, and put it with the fat into an enamelled saucepan. Add the chopped mushroom, thyme, parsley, shallot, &c., and fry it all over the fire for a time. If the mass is too dry, it shows there is not enough bacon-fat; if it is too moist, add some bread-crumbs. Next fill the cups of the mushrooms with this preparation, and shake some fine golden-coloured bread-raspings. Place these cups in a covered stew-pan with some butter or oil, and let them cook very gently till the cup part of the mushroom is quite tender. They can be served either plain or with some rich brown gravy poured *round* them. It is rather a rich dish, and of course not one off which it would be possible to dine; but it is exceedingly good and savoury, and not nearly so troublesome to make as would be imagined from reading this recipe.

Should these mushrooms *au gratin* be required as an entrée, where great excellence is desirable, an improvement will be found by adding two yolks of eggs to the mass after it has been taken off the fire. These yolks must be stirred in thoroughly, and have the effect of rendering the insides of the mushrooms richer in appearance and taste. They are not, however, in my opinion, necessary.

When there has been a large lobster salad or salads made, the cook is often at a loss how to utilise the lobster that is left. In the first place, lobster will not keep sometimes even one hot night. One very good method of using up any remains is what is called bashawed lobster. Take all the pieces of lobster left, and cut them up with a knife and fork; chop up a little piece of onion, about the size of the top of the little finger, and a small piece of parsley. Mix it with the pieces of lobster, and a very little anchovy sauce and cayenne pepper. Cut up a piece of butter into little pieces, and mix in, and fill the shell part of the lobster—*i.e.*, the two half-tails. Cover these shells over the top with some fine bread-crumbs, and shake a few fine bread-raspings on the top. Put the shells in the oven for ten minutes, or a little longer, and serve hot. Some fried parsley makes a good garnish in contrast with the red shell, and is also a great improvement to the flavour. This is a capital supper dish after a hot day, can be made early in the afternoon, and only requires what the cooks call "popping in the oven."

Cook will, of course, maintain that the remains of a lobster or lobsters cannot be done this way properly. The reason is, lobster—and, in fact, shell-fish generally—has particular charms for the kitchen. Servants are partial also to cucumber, vinegar, liver and bacon, lamb's fry, roast pork and sage-and-onions, winkles, radishes, &c.—almost anything with stuffing, onions—in fact, generally it may be said that anything that possesses what is vulgarly known as the property of rising seems adapted to them. They invariably dislike calve's heads, and cold boiled beef, or, in fact, any cold meat, especially Australian. Like Mrs. Gamp, they scorn hash, but somehow like stewed steak, both dishes affording admirable opportunities for displays of dexterity with the blade of the knife.

The world, thanks to strikes, trades-unions, love of dress, drink, &c., is changing very rapidly. Where the class of servants is to come from ten years hence, adapted to small families of limited incomes, is a problem to be solved in the future.

XIII.—COOLING DRINKS.

WHAT subject is so suitable for early summer? Who has not at times experienced that strange and almost painful feeling that must exist in the throat in order that the sensation may be worthy of the name of "thirst?" I recollect many years ago either hearing or reading a horrible story of the refinement of cruelty. A prisoner is supposed to have been lowered into a deep dungeon, and to have been left for a whole day without food. Ravenous with hunger, what are his feelings on seeing the dungeon-top unclosed, and slowly lowered a silver dish containing probably food. The dish is at length grasped and uncovered, and is found to contain some bread and nicely cooked salt fish, both of which are eagerly devoured. The dish is slowly drawn up, and the prisoner left alone. What, however, were the pains of hunger that he felt, compared to the raging thirst he now experiences, a thirst greatly increased by the nature of the food he has eaten—viz., salt fish! Another twenty-four hours of agony, tenfold greater than he experienced before, pass heavily away, and again the dungeon opens, and a large and beautiful silver goblet is seen slowly to descend, and sends a quiver of hope through the frame of the poor agonised wretch, almost raving. The goblet is at length clutched, somewhat like a drowning man would clutch a straw. Alas! the goblet is found to be empty, and he is left to Death, more merciful than his gaolers.

Horrible stories, too, have been told of travellers in the desert, who, in their death-agony, have ripped open and ladled out a spoonful or two of water from their camel's stomach.

However, we live in a happier clime; certain is it that should any one experience thirst in this country, it is not for want of opportunities to drink.

Before, however, we proceed to discuss the various methods and recipes for cooling drinks, such as claret-cup, champagne-cup, as well as home-made lemonade, lemon-smash, &c., it will not be out of place to compare (as we have already done in cooking) France and England, in regard to drinking. If it is urged there is a good old saying that "comparisons are odious," we would add, so also is drunkenness. That this latter vice is the curse of the country, and has been for many years, no one will deny. That of late private tippling in families far above the lower orders is also on the increase, is a fact so patent that it deserves more notice than that it has hitherto met with in purely medical journals.

Perhaps one of the simplest and most effective cures for the dangerous habit we speak of is the substitution of some agreeable but at the same time harmless drink, for the usual stimulant.

We believe that this point has not met with the attention it deserves. The public-houses of London are essentially drinking-houses. A poor man, to whom every penny is an object, is almost driven when thirsty to take beer—too often, unfortunately, the beer in question being so adulterated that it helps in the end to increase rather than alleviate thirst. On the other hand, a Paris café contains a choice of drinks almost unknown in London, many of which combine a delicious flavour with the advantage of being non-intoxicating. I have known several cases of English lads who, when in England, invariably took beer, who looked forward with pleasure to the equally cheap glass of groseille and water when abroad. These to whom I refer were in charge of some race-horses, had been educated at Newmarket, and were constantly in the habit of travelling between that place and Paris.

Young lads at the dangerous and susceptible age of seventeen too often take to drinking more beer than is good for them, just in the same way that they take to smoking—viz., because they think it will look manly, and not because they really like it. The habit once formed, in nine cases out of ten probably lasts a lifetime; but the good old saying, that "prevention is better than cure," was never more applicable than in the case in point.

We could recommend some enterprising grocers during the present summer to offer for sale glasses of syrup and water—say groseille—with a small piece of ice in each glass, for a penny; the profit would be considerable. Were every grocer's shop in London to adopt this suggestion, I believe more would be done towards checking intemperance than all the efforts of the teetotal societies have done for years.

There are several ways of making claret-cup, and many persons have their own private recipe. It will also invariably be found that each person thinks his own recipe the best. In this respect claret-cup may be said to have taken the place of punch, disputes about the best method of brewing a bowl of which are said in days of old to have even led to duels being fought between the rival brewers.

I will give two recipes for making claret-cup—one, which may be called strong cup, suitable for dinner, and another weaker cup, more adapted to be drunk after cricket or rowing. There are, perhaps, few occasions when a deep draught of a cool fluid is more grateful than after a long pull on the river on a hot day.

Of course the basis of claret-cup is claret; but one

word of warning somewhat similar to that we gave in connection with turtle soup. It is impossible to make a good cup out of really bad claret. I do not mean cheap claret, but sour. It is quite possible to get a good sound wine for twenty-four shillings a dozen, or even less; but at the same time it is quite possible to pay more, and get a sour compound that would be unfit for cup or any other purpose. On the other hand, to use really good claret, such as Château Margaux or Château Latour, for making cup, would be as bad as using 1834 port to make negus.

Perhaps the most difficult point to determine in making claret-cup is its sweetness. Now, as this is purely a matter of taste, I would recommend persons to err on the side of too little sugar rather than too much, as it is always easy to add, but impossible to take away.

Take therefore about an ounce and a half of white sugar, and dissolve it by pouring a table-spoonful of hot water on it, and afterwards adding a little claret. I have always found this plan best, as otherwise the sugar is apt to settle at the bottom of the cup or jug, thereby often making the compound not quite sweet enough at starting, and a great deal too sweet at the finish.

We will suppose, therefore, that the sugar is completely dissolved, and added to a whole bottle of claret in the jug or cup selected for the purpose. Add two thin slices of lemon—cut across the lemon, care being taken to avoid any pips—and one thin slice of cucumber-peeling about as long and as broad as the first finger, and the thickness of the blade of a dinner-knife. Next add one sherry-glassful of sherry, one table-spoonful of *good* brandy—not some of that dreadful cheap brandy that smells like naphtha—and one table-spoonful of noyeau or maraschino. Rub a nutmeg about half a dozen times across the grater over the cup.

Let the cup stand for about a quarter of an hour, and then taste it. Should the flavour of the cucumber be very decided, take out the piece of cucumber; and the same as regards the lemon. Should the flavour of the peel of the lemon be detected, take out the two slices of lemon, for lemons vary immensely in strength.

Now add a large lump of ice and a bottle of soda-water, taking care to pour the latter in carefully—*i.e.*, to put the soda-water bottle almost into the cup. I have seen persons pour the soda water from a height, thereby losing half the carbonic-acid gas, which ought to go into the cup to freshen it up, so to speak.

All that the cup now requires is drinking. It is by no means a very cheap affair, as the sherry, brandy, and noyeau probably cost more than the claret.

A cheaper form of cup, and one more suitable for use, as we have said, after cricket or rowing, is a bottle of claret with the same quantity of lemon, cucumber-peel, and sugar, two or three drops of essence of almonds, a large lump of ice, and two bottles of soda-water.

One word, however, in reference to the lemon proper not only for claret-cup, but for any other kind of cup. The lemon must be fresh—*i.e.*, when it is cut it must have a firm rim round it, yellow outside and white inside. An old lemon, that is soft and pulpy, with a hard, dry skin, and that smells sweet, is no good for claret-cup. In making champagne-cup it is still more important to have a good lemon.

The method of making champagne-cup that I think best is so simple that it barely deserves the name of a recipe. It is as follows:—A bottle of champagne, one or two thin slices of lemon, a large lump of ice, and a bottle of soda-water.

Francatelli is, however, so great an authority in cooking, and all his recipes, so far as cooking is concerned, so invariably correct, that I will give his recipe for making both champagne and claret-cup, merely remarking that I have not tried either. Francatelli recommends—" One bottle of champagne, one quart bottle of German seltzer-water, two oranges sliced, a bunch of balm, ditto of burrage, one ounce of bruised sugar-candy. Place the ingredients in a covered jug embedded in rough ice for an hour and a quarter previously to its being required for use, and then decanter it free from the herbs, &c." I should think the fault in this cup would be that it would taste too sweet.

For claret-cup Francatelli recommends—"One bottle of claret, one pint bottle of German seltzer water, a small bunch of balm and burrage, one orange cut in slices, half a cucumber sliced thick, a liqueur-glass of cognac, and one ounce of bruised sugar-candy. Place these ingredients in a covered jug well immersed in rough ice. Stir all together with a silver spoon, and when the cup has been iced for about an hour, strain or decanter it off free from the herbs, &c." In this recipe I should think there would be far too strong a flavour of cucumber.

One of the most refreshing drinks in very hot weather is lemonade; but how rare is it that we meet with lemonade that is really nice! Of course tastes differ, but I cannot understand how some people can drink the ordinary bottled lemonade. It is, as a rule, so very sweet that it is absolutely sickly, and at the same time in such a state of effervescence that only peculiarly constituted throats can drink it at a draught. Plain home-made lemonade can be made very cheaply, when lemons are not too dear. The great secret is to use boiling water, and pour it on the pulp of, say, three lemons, with a small piece of peel, but not too much, as it will render the lemonade bitter. Add white sugar to taste ; of course, children like it sweeter than others. Let it get cold, and then strain it. Care should be taken that all the pips are removed from the pulp before the boiling water is added. A great improvement to this kind of lemonade is the addition of a little *dilute sulphuric acid*, about thirty drops to a quart. Thirty drops of dilute sulphuric acid, when freely diluted, can be taken at one dose without any fear, though of course such a dose must not be taken without a doctor's order ; but the addition of it to a whole quart of lemonade has the effect of rendering it much more palatable ; and were a person to drink the whole quart, which is improbable, it would not do them the slightest possible harm. Dilute sulphuric acid is a simple but valuable medicine, particularly useful in summer.

Those who prefer sparkling lemonade had better try the following method, and then let them judge for themselves whether it is not infinitely superior to the ordinary bottled lemonade :—Squeeze a lemon through a little piece of muslin into a tumbler, and have the patience to wait while a couple of lumps of sugar dissolve in it. Then add some iced soda-water and stir it up, taking care it is not half lost by frothing over the tumbler.

Soda-water can be bought now very good at one shilling and ninepence a dozen. Mixed with a little fruit-essence or French syrup, or raspberry vinegar, it makes most delicious drinks, especially if iced. Let me, therefore, entreat ladies who, during this hot weather, when they feel at times exhausted, have been in the habit of taking either weak brandy-and-water or sherry-and-water, to try one of these kinds of syrup instead. The effect of a stimulant is but short, and too often is followed by a reaction far worse than the original feeling of lassitude.

There is one subject in connection with cooling drinks that I wish to mention, though a trifle out of place in an article that purports teaching cooking; yet its importance is so great that I trust I may be pardoned for introducing it. When you use water for drinking, or for mixing cooling drinks, take care that it is pure. No house ought to be without a filter. Were the custom of first boiling and then filtering water universal, tens of thousands of lives would be annually saved throughout the country. Children are peculiarly susceptible to the influence of impure water, and during hot weather especially drink a great deal. The cost of a filter is small, and the trouble of boiling the water also small.

Let me strongly advise mothers in small households, where no trustworthy housekeeper is kept, to superintend the management of the filter themselves. If my advice be the means of saving the life of even one little one, it will not have been given in vain. Should any one say or think that this is all rubbish, let that one ask any respectable medical man for his opinion, and then act on it.

XIV.—GAME AND GRAVY.

"The month 'tis now September; the season has begun when English customs give us game, when dinner's almost done." Now for my own part I think we often rather waste our game in this country, by bringing it in when really everybody has dined; or if some one has what may be called reserved himself, he probably finds he gets such an exceedingly small portion that he runs considerable risk of going home hungry.

I recollect an old story of a notorious gourmand, who was asked to dine with a so-called friend, who played upon him the following cruel practical joke— A little soup and fish was followed by a plain leg of mutton, and the gourmand was informed that he saw his dinner before him. He accordingly gorged freely, while his host scarcely tasted a mouthful. The leg of mutton was, however, followed by a splendid haunch of venison.

"It was cruel not to tell me," said the guest, with tears of anguish rolling down his cheeks.

The story does not sound like a true one, and we trust for the sake of human nature it is not; but it exemplifies our point in saying, or rather asking, is it not a mistake when game is cheap and plentiful, to leave it quite to the last?

I must say I admire the good, honest English hospitality of the North. It may be called the Black Country, but as long as black is associated with blackcock and grouse, long may it remain so.

Nowhere do you get grouse in such perfection as in the neighbourhood of the moors. They have not yet arrived at that depraved state of appetite in which it is considered the right thing to send game to table nearly putrid; nor, as a rule, do you get one, or at the outside two, mouthfuls put on your plate by an elegant waiter. Elegant waiters are all very well in their way, but we prefer grouse.

Now game, whether grouse, partridge, pheasant, or woodcock, requires careful cooking, and, above all things, good gravy.

By good gravy we mean that which will assist, and not counteract or destroy, the flavour of the game. Weak beef-tea or rich turtle soup would be alike wrong; and it will, we fear, be too often found that cooks fail very much in adapting the gravy to the occasion. Roast goose with sage-and-onion stuffing would bear a gravy which, so to speak, would kill the delicate flavour of a partridge.

Game served as a salmi, which nine times out of

K

ten means game cooked before and warmed up, requires quite a differently-flavoured sauce to game proper—*i.e.*, game, not too fresh, and at the same time not at all high, roasted to a turn and served quickly.

In cooking game I fear we cannot learn much from that nation of cooks, the French. I am such an admirer of French cooking as a rule, that I wish to speak with the greatest diffidence, but did you ever taste any game, never mind of what kind, at any foreign hotel or restaurant abroad, to compare with the game we get at home?

I say hotel or restaurant, as I have had no experience of French country private houses.

Whether this is owing to the game itself being of inferior quality or flavour—as is undoubtedly the case with red-legged partridges, when compared with the ordinary English ones—or to other causes, I cannot say, but simply record the fact.

There is no doubt that a large class of men enjoy their food when game is in season more than at any other time.

The class to whom we refer are those who live for the greater part of the year in London, and as a rule never move a mile except in a hansom; to such the 12th of August is the commencement of what may be termed their annual training, the exercise they take during the next three months probably saving them from the inevitable gout and dyspepsia which would necessarily follow a town life such as theirs without such intervals.

What a change! First the early rising—and there are thousands whom nothing but hunting or shooting will persuade to get up early—the substantial breakfast, the glass of bitter, the gun examination, the struggle into the heavy greased shooting-boots, and then the tramp through the heather. What with the exercise and the bracing air of the moors, lunch is approached with feelings which by contrast approximate to what we should imagine the alderman's would have been, had he carried out the famous doctor's recipe—viz., to live on a shilling a day, and earn it.

Let us hope the hungry sportsmen may not meet with the disappointment that occurred to a shooting-party on the moors, that we referred to before. The first brace of grouse shot were sent to a neighbouring farm to be cooked for lunch. The farmer's wife, however, had them *boiled*, and stuffed with sage and onions.

There are various ways of cooking grouse, but only one which we consider to be worthy of consideration, and that is what we term grouse *au naturel*, or in other words plain roast, with good gravy and fried bread-crumbs, or bread sauce.

To overpower the delicious flavour of a good grouse with strong sauces seems to us as cruel a waste as to mull good 1848 La Fitte claret, and mix in cinnamon and sugar.

As an instance, however, of what cooks may come to, we will mention an Italian method of spoiling grouse—the ingredients for this extraordinary dish comprising mace, garlic, brandy, macaroni, tomato sauce, and Parmesan cheese. Imagine what a dish this Italian cook and our farmer's wife could manufacture between them!

The first point to be considered with regard to game is, How long should it be kept?

When game is bought, it is of course impossible to say how long it has been killed, except from appearances. As a rule, the first symptom of discolouring, or the faintest smell of being high, shows that the birds are ripe for cooking. We would, however, allow a pheasant a longer time than either a partridge or a grouse. A thoroughly fresh pheasant is more tough than a fowl.

Game, in fact, should be treated exactly like a good haunch of mutton. No one would keep a haunch till it is *high*, but yet every one knows that the longer it is kept the more tender it becomes. In a large number of London shops the game for sale has already been kept too long, reminding one of the story of the man who arrived home after a days' shooting, who had, however, been driven to buy a brace for appearances, the look of which called forth the remark from his wife—

"Well, my dear, it is time they were shot, for they are getting very high."

The next point to be considered is the actual cooking. We will suppose the birds ready trussed. They should be wiped inside, but never washed.

All game requires a brisk fire, and plenty of basting. It is the custom among French cooks to fasten a thin slice of bacon over the breast, in order to prevent the bird being too dry. Indeed, they go so far as to send the bird to table with the bacon still on. In my opinion, this spoils the flavour of the bird altogether, giving it what may be termed a greasy taste. If bacon is fastened on at all, it should be taken off before the bird is taken down; the breast should then be basted with a little butter, and frothed and browned before it is sent up.

With regard to the time that it takes to cook game, it is difficult to lay down any general rule. The time of course varies with the size of the birds. Young, small partridges want about twenty-five minutes; good-sized partridges as much as thirty-five minutes; small grouse will take a little over half an hour, and good-sized ones require three-quarters; pheasants require from thirty-five minutes to an hour; or even more, according to the size.

The principal thing, however, for the cook to bear in mind is to adapt the time to the period of dinner when the game will be required. Herein lies the great secret of game being badly cooked. Have you not often at a large dinner-party had game completely dried up, the outside skin being quite hard? The reason of this is that the game was ready for table about the period you were finishing your soup. The fact is, cooks, especially young and inexperienced, get nervous about time, forgetting that it is quite as bad to have things dried up as to have them underdone. It would be a good plan were the housekeeper to give the following directions to the cook:—Do not begin to cook the game until you send up the soup. Suppose the dinner to consist of soup, fish, entrées, and joint, followed by game, there is ample time to cook grouse, or even a small pheasant, by putting them down as soon as the soup is served. In any case tell the cook never to put down game until they know that dinner may be served. The late arrival of some important guest should never be the excuse of overcooked game. It would be far better to have a slight pause in the middle of the dinner than to have things spoilt. Besides, a pause after soup, fish, entrées, and joint is never objectionable.

Another important point is the basting. Game should be basted directly it is put down. Ordinary dripping is quite good enough to commence with, but it will be found an improvement if during the last five minutes a little butter is used instead. Baste quickly with a little butter, and froth it at the same time, shaking a little fine dried flour over the breast out of a flour-dredger. When this is done, let the game be sent up immediately. Treat it, in fact, like a soufflé, which everybody knows, or ought to know, requires a running-man for a waiter to be served properly.

In making bread sauce, it will be generally found that cooks make it a long time before dinner—in fact, putting in the bread-crumbs, so to speak, to soak in a saucepan, with an onion, in a little milk. The result often is that the milk all dries up, and the sauce gets burnt; a fresh lot has to be made in a hurry, and a sort of bread poultice is sent to table. There is, however, a good deal of difference between bread sauce and a bread poultice. The way to make the former is as follows :—Have ready some dry bread-crumbs, put these in some milk, or, still better, cream, and boil them, with an onion and a few peppercorns, for about ten minutes; take out the onion, add a pinch of salt, and a little butter, keep stirring till the butter is dissolved and well mixed in; add, if you like, a suspicion of nutmeg, and the sauce is finished. Take care in taking out the onion that it does not break, as it is extremely disagreeable to have a piece of onion left in the sauce; it is apt to get into the mouth by mistake, and give notice of its presence by a crunch which is not at all pleasant.

With regard to gravy for game, what is required is that it should be good and strong, yet without any predominant flavour. For instance, some cooks like to add mushroom ketchup to gravy. This, when the gravy is intended for roast goose or fowl, would be unobjectionable, but should certainly be avoided when the gravy is intended for game. Again, the flavour of garlic should be guarded against. There is an old proverb which says, "It is a pity to spoil the ship for a ha'p'orth of tar." So, too, it is a pity to spoil a brace of grouse for the sake of a little gravy-beef, and recollect a little and good is better than plenty and poor. Equal quantities of good gravy-beef and knuckle of veal should be used; of course, less gravy-beef is necessary when extract of meat is used. The gravy may be thickened with a little brown thickening, but not too much. A very little arrowroot may be used, but the gravy for game should be by no means thick, yet at the same time it should look of a rich dark colour.

To make a salmi of game. It is almost always the case that the game has been previously cooked. Take, therefore, any game-bones or trimmings that can be got, and place them, with a bay-leaf, to stew as long as possible in some gravy similar to what we have described, which is simply good strong stock made from gravy-beef, knuckle of veal stewed with an onion in which a few cloves have been stuck, a head of celery, a carrot and turnip, and a large handful of parsley, flavoured with pepper and salt, &c. After stewing all the game-bones, you can strain off the gravy from them and the bay-leaf; make the gravy a trifle thicker with a little more brown thickening; make this gravy hot in a stew-pan and then add the remains of the game, cut off as neatly as possible; let it soak in the gravy, but do not let it boil; about a quarter of an hour before serving, add a wine-glassful of madeira, or good golden sherry. A pale dry sherry is not nearly so good for the purpose. It is really the addition of the wine that makes the gravy into the salmi sauce—just as in nearly all the French restaurants in London it will often be seen in the bill of fare, something with sauce Madère, which simply means some ordinary gravy to which has been added a spoonful of sherry.

To make fried bread-crumbs—the best accompaniment to grouse—a clear fire is necessary. Get an enamelled stew-pan, and put a little butter in it (about an ounce), then get some bread-crumbs, stale and not too fine, throw them in the butter, aud keep stirring till they begin to change colour; as soon as they do, remove the stewpan from the fire, but keep on stirring; the process of cooking, as we have said before, goes on some time after the stew-pan is removed. As soon as they are sufficiently brown, place them on some blotting-paper, in order that all the grease may be soaked up.

The blotting-paper can be placed in front of the fire, and the bread-crumbs tossed lightly about with a fork. The bread-crumbs can be made hot in the oven when required for use, but should not be allowed to remain in too long, as they are apt to get too hard and crisp, and thereby get converted into tooth-breakers.

As we have said before, game, at any rate in this country, is far too good a thing to be left to the last, and then to be brought forward only in mouthfuls. The fact is, we are all of us to a great extent creatures of habit. We, as a rule, do what other people do, without reasoning whether it is right or wrong, good or bad, but simply because we shrink from drawing out a line for ourselves, or because we fear to be thought eccentric. For instance, take an ordinary party of, say, ten persons at dinner at the present season. We cling to soup, fish, entrées, and joint, and follow it up with game, served in the same course with sweets, the latter often being expensive to make, and uncared for by the majority. Suppose we change our dinner into, first, a little good clear soup; secondly, a good haunch of mutton, well kept and well cooked, and let this be followed by some game in sufficient quantity. When we are by ourselves, we own probably we could manage half a grouse after " a cut off the joint." Why therefore not save the money too often wasted over second-rate entrées and sweets intended more to please the eye than the palate, and spend it in giving a dinner which, if not quite in the fashion, will at any rate please?

Were this done, you may be certain of one point, that your house will be considered one at which it is worth while dining.

A glass of Pomerey and Grem's champagne, cold, but not frozen, at dinner, followed by a good bottle of claret, say Château Margeaux (which may be placed on a top shelf in the kitchen during the day to bring out its flavour), after dinner, will have the effect of sending home your guests enabled to say from their hearts, or at any rate their stomachs, "I have dined."

HOW TO COOK HARE.

ONCE again has that season come round in which earth appears to be most lavish in her gifts to men. In our own country may be seen miles of ground on which rich golden grain waves in the autumn sun, waiting for the reaper's hook, while in the present age, when the iron horse almost annihilates both time and distance, within a few hours' journey from our shores may be seen that glorious sight where the earth seems reeling with rich purple profusion soon to be converted into the wine that "cheereth God and man." As often happens, with change of season also comes change of food, a change doubly welcome in a country like our own, which seems to possess fewer changes than others, on the beef and mutton, mutton and beef, day after day and week after week. There are, perhaps, few changes more decided than that of hare in the shape of food, and few dishes that persons would care less to eat every day. Still, it is a change, and a pleasant one; but hare requires rather more skill in cooking than many cooks are aware of. Hare really properly cooked has simply to be compared with hare carelessly served to prove the truth of this statement.

I will begin by describing that simple dish, roast hare. Now what is the common fault to be found with this excellent dish, as we get it in nine houses out of ten? It is nearly always dried up, that part of the meat of the back which in roasting is nearest the fire seems covered with a thick, hard skin, the reason being that it has roasted too long, too fast, and has not been sufficiently basted. In cooking hare, and, in fact, in cooking any kind of meat, the nature of that meat should be borne in mind. The specialty about hare is that it has a tendency to taste what we may call dry; and also, it possesses very little natural fat. Consequently the cook's great object should be to keep the hare as moist as possible, and to prevent it from getting dry. In all high-class works on cooking, entrées made from hare are invariably spoken of as larded fillets, which are finished by the addition of various sauces, &c.; but I do not think it would be very practical to describe the process of larding fillets of hare. Larding requires practice, and one practical lesson of *seeing* it done would be worth a volume of bulk—indeed I might as well attempt to explain how to shoot the hare; I fear the cook who depended upon "reading" for her knowledge of larding would miss her mark, as surely as the sportsman whose sole experience consisted of a similar kind would miss his.

There is an old saying, "A disease once known is half-cured;" the disease, so to speak, against which we have to contend is dryness. In roasting a hare, therefore, bear in mind the importance of basting, and also of not letting the hare be too close to the fire in the early stage of roasting. But to begin at the beginning: We will suppose the hare caught and hung up, head downwards, in his fur jacket. Now the first thing to be thought of is the length of time that a hare should be kept before it is cooked. This entirely depends upon the weather; a perfectly fresh hare should never be cooked unless the whole of it is intended for hare-soup, which is rarely the case save in small private houses. Some persons prefer the hare absolutely high; the best course is a happy medium between being too high and too fresh, and cooks should bear in mind that what often appears very high and offensive when raw, becomes perfectly right when cooked.

We will not dwell upon that not very agreeable but still necessary process of skinning the hare, but will at once commence to make the stuffing, which must be tied up inside it. Ordinary veal stuffing, as it is generally called, is best for the purpose, and, as I think I have before pointed out, the most common fault is too much lemon.

The following recipe will, I think, be found well adapted to improve, and not destroy or overcome, the flavour of the hare:—Take $\frac{1}{4}$ lb. of beef suet, and chop it very finely, with 2 oz. of raw lean ham; add a tea-spoonful of chopped fresh parsley and 2 tea-spoonfuls of dried mixed savoury herbs, or 1, if these savoury herbs are fresh. These herbs are sold ready mixed, in bottles, which is the simplest method, and are composed principally of marjoram, basil, thyme, &c. As the herbs get drier, more must be used, but, as I have said, if quite fresh, 1 tea-spoonful; if very dry, 2; the cook consequently must use her judgment for intermediate stages. Add to this, to continue the stuffing, ¼ of the rind of a lemon (this latter should be chopped very fine); add a little cayenne pepper and salt, about 5 oz. of bread-crumbs, and 2 whole eggs. The whole quantity should be well pounded in a mortar.

Some persons add the liver of the hare to the stuffing; if the liver is quite fresh this may be done, but not unless; and if the hare has been kept a proper time, the liver is very often the part that exhibits most the—what shall we call it?—ravages of time, and in such case should on no account be used. This stuffing must be placed in the hare, taking care to wipe the inside first, and sewn up; the hare should then be hung up before the fire, at a greater distance than meat would be ordinarily; plenty of dripping should be ready melted in the dripping-pan, and the cook should *keep basting as often as possible;* this latter is the secret of having the hare moist, and without that hard dry coating outside which we mentioned. As for the time a hare takes to roast, it is almost impossible to say—a small one taking an hour, and a very large one nearly two. Much depends, also, on the fire, and the distance the hare is kept from it in the early stages. Bear in mind, however, that underdone can be remedied, and overdone can't. An inexperienced cook can cut into the joint at the back, about where the hind-leg joins the body, and look; or stick a little piece of firewood in after the knife, and judge by the colour whether it is done or not. On the average, an hour to an hour and a quarter will be ample. Near the finish, however, take away the dripping-pan and get a little butter; baste the hare with this to finish, putting the hare near the fire so as to froth the butter, and at the same time dredge the hare with some flour, so as to get it a nice brown-colour, and serve some good rich, hot gravy with it in a separate tureen. As hare is an awkward joint to carve, it will be found best *not* to pour gravy over it, for the sake of the tablecloth and the feelings of the carver. Red-currant jelly should always be handed round with hare, and the gravy will be much improved by a few cloves, a tiny piece of cinnamon being boiled in it and then strained off; add also half a glass of rich port wine, and by rich I mean not a dry wine, but rather port-wine dregs. The last spoonful of port in the bottle should always be reserved for purposes of this kind.

We will now discuss what is, to my mind, a far preferable method of cooking hare, and that is, jugged hare. For this purpose a stone jar with a wide mouth will be found to be better than an ordinary jug, which used to be used, and which gives its name to the dish. Have ready some good brown gravy, free from fat. Next cut up the hare into joints, each joint not being larger than would be considered the proper quantity for one help; fry these joints in a little butter in a frying-pan, so as to turn them a nice brown without cooking them. Have the empty jar made hot by placing it in the oven, and have a cloth ready to tie over its mouth. Then as soon as the joints of hare are browned, throw them into the hot empty jar, pour a large glass of port wine in too, and tie the cloth quickly over the mouth of the jar, and let it stand for, say, a quarter of an hour or more, on the dresser. By this means the fumes of the wine will rise—the jar being hot—and will impregnate the meat of the hare in a way in which it would never do were it simply added to the gravy. After this has stood some time, untie the jar and add the gravy, with a small piece of cinnamon, six cloves, two bay-leaves, and the juice of half a lemon. The gravy should be strongly impregnated with onion, and should be thickened with a little arrowroot rather than with brown thickening. The port will materially assist the colour; a good spoonful of red-currant jelly may also be added to it and dissolved in it, though in addition red-currant jelly will be handed round with it. Next place this jar up to its neck in a large saucepan of boiling water, only take care that the jar is well tied down, or much of the flavour will be lost; allow this to remain in the boiling water for about an hour to an hour and a half, when it will be found to be sufficiently done, as jugged hare, like roast hare, is generally over-cooked rather than under. Stuffing-balls should be added to it, but not cooked with it. For this purpose prepare some stuffing as directed for roast hare. Roll this stuffing into small balls, a little larger than marbles, and throw them into some boiling fat. A few minutes will be sufficient to cook them; drain them on a cloth and make them hot in the oven before adding them to the jugged hare.

As I before mentioned, hare soup is best made from fresh hare, in which case as much as possible of the blood of the hare should be preserved, and used in the soup. However, it will be often found expedient to use up the remains of the jugged hare by converting it into hare soup for the following day. I will proceed to explain the best method of doing this: —First you must have ready some really good stock; next pick out all the best-looking pieces of meat—little slices from the back are best—and put them by on a plate, to be added to the soup at the last moment; next take all the remains of the hare, add it to the stock with, if possible, a head of celery; let it all boil for an hour or more, till the celery is quite tender, strain off the meat, take out carefully all the bones, which will be found after this boiling to be quite white and dry, and then, with a good-sized wooden spoon, rub all the meat and celery through a wire sieve into the stock. This will take time; but recollect, the one secret of good hare soup is the fact of the meat of the hare being rubbed through the sieve helping to make the soup not only thicker, but materially affecting the taste. Indeed, I may go farther, and say the excellence of the soup is in proportion to the amount of hare-flesh rubbed through the sieve. Should, therefore, the soup look a little thin, allow it to boil away and decrease in quantity. Of course, the taste will much depend upon the amount of jugged hare left; but a little port wine may be added at the finish, as the flavour of wine in soups is very apt to go off after they have been boiled for any length of time. A little more lemon-juice may be added near the finish, but avoid putting in too much currant jelly. Some persons think hare soup should be absolutely sweet. For my part, I think this a mistake; besides, red-currant jelly can always be added if wished, but cannot be taken out of the soup. The soup should be made slightly thicker by means of brown thickening, which I have before described to be simply butter and flour fried of a rich brown colour. Do not, however, use too much of this thickening, as it will be found to somewhat destroy the delicate flavour of the hare; besides which, good hare soup should by no means be very thick. It will, however, have one very marked effect, and that is, it will enable you to add some more port wine, or port-wine dregs, which has such an enormous influence over the flavour of hare soup. When the soup is about to be served, throw in the little slices of hare that had been put by on the plate, but do not let the soup boil, as the hare is probably already more than cooked by being jugged. Allow, therefore, these pieces of meat to remain in the soup just long enough to get hot, and no longer. One objection brought against jugged hare and hare soup is the quantity of port wine evidently required in order that the result should be worthy of the trouble bestowed. Recollect, however, what I have said with regard to port-wine dregs. Now there are many homes where port wine is had in in the shape of a quarter-cask; where this is the case there should be no difficulty, if the precaution is taken to bottle the thick dregs of the wine and reserve them. Port is, however, a wine, I am sorry to say, going out of fashion; still, good, decent, sound burgundy will do nearly as well for cooking, and in the Burgundy district in France nothing else is ever used; indeed, so far claret may be used, and considering how nice a sauce bordelaise is, I should imagine would do very well, especially as all French cookery-books, in giving directions as to cooking hare, simply say, add red wine. When claret or burgundy is used instead of port, I would recommend the addition of a little, a very little, nutmeg, and also a little extra red-currant jelly, for, bear in mind, port is sweeter than claret.

XV.—FOOD FOR COLD WEATHER.

There can be no doubt that we live in an exceedingly variable climate, and for by far the greater part of the year we suffer neither the extreme of heat nor cold. Still we have at times our hot July or August days, when the English summer, which is often described as consisting of three hot days and a thunderstorm, vies with almost any heat that can be met with in the whole continent of Europe.

Fortunately for the present season of the year, we are, as a nation, far better prepared to resist the attacks of cold than heat.

Abundant—though now, alas! not cheap—coal is to be obtained, and feather-beds, thick blankets, carpeted rooms, are the universal custom in this country—making a winter in London as far superior to one in Paris as a summer in the latter city is superior to one in London.

The question, however, before us is, Do we as a nation sufficiently vary our food to make it consistent with the weather? Here, again, I must confess that we are more apt to give winter's food in summer-time than summer's food in winter. Still there are certain dishes especially adapted for cold weather, and at the present season of the year we may call attention to some of them. First, however, it may not be amiss to consider on what general principles one kind of food is adapted for hot countries and another for cold. The first principle is to remember that in cold weather we require *fat*. Fat and grease contain a large quantity of carbon, and this carbon taken and absorbed into the system keeps up the animal heat.

There is an old story told that many years ago, when the streets of London were lighted with oil-lamps, before the introduction of gas, Russian sailors in England were in the habit of climbing the lamps and drinking the lamp-oil. It is also asserted that in some of the Arctic expeditions the sailors have boiled down and eaten the tallow candles.

Whether these stories are true or not may be left an open question, but there is no doubt that the food craved for was that best suited to sustain heat. We all know how invaluable a remedy cod-liver oil has proved to many invalids, especially among young children, and how medical men often recommend cod-liver oil to delicate persons, to be taken during the winter, and left off on the return of warm spring weather.

Now, of all winter dishes, perhaps none is so suitable for cold weather as that rather vulgar dish, pea-soup.

Persons who affect to despise pea-soup should remember that it is one of the most variable soups ever made. Poor pea-soup, which really owes almost its whole goodness to the split-peas from which it is made, is indeed poor stuff for epicures, though a very cheap and wholesome form of nourishment for the hungry poor. Good pea-soup is an exceedingly delicious compound, and I will describe how to make it.

First of all, one great advantage of pea-soup is that a greasy stock, scarcely adapted to make any other kind of soup, is really best suited for the purpose. For instance, the water in which a large piece of pickled pork has been boiled, or even the greasy water in which ham or bacon has been boiled, is admirably adapted for making pea-soup. As a rule, the water used for boiling salt beef is too salt to be used for making soup; however, very often by soaking a piece of salt beef in fresh water for twenty-four hours before boiling it, the liquor left will be found to be not too salt for making pea-soup—the cook of course remembering that no further salt is added.

We will suppose, therefore, that some stock, or rather some greasy liquor, has been left, say in quantity about two quarts; and I would here suggest that the water in which, say, a piece of fresh silverside of beef has been boiled, should be used again to boil, say, a good-sized piece of bacon, that may be eaten hot with some roast fowls one day, and afterwards left as a cold breakfast-dish. First of all, take a quart of split peas and put them into a large basin, and let them soak in fresh water for nearly a day, a little piece of soda rather bigger than a pea being put into the water, to render it softer. Should any of the peas float on the water, take them off and throw them away. Next, strain off these peas, and put them in the greasy stock mentioned to boil, and add to the two quarts of liquor one good-sized head of celery, four good-sized onions, two carrots, two turnips, and a little parsley. Let all this boil till the whole is thoroughly soft, occasionally skimming the soup, taking off that nasty thick film of fat which will occasionally rise to the surface. When the peas are thoroughly soft, strain the whole through a wire sieve into a large basin; pick out the stalk of the parsley, and with a good-sized wooden spoon rub the whole through the wire sieve.

This is the great secret of good soup. Too often the cook will not take the trouble to send the whole through the sieve. It is undoubtedly a troublesome affair, and very apt to make the wrist ache. However, the result well repays the trouble, and the cook generally can call some one to her assistance to take a turn with the spoon. It will also be found advisable every now and then to moisten the ingredients in the sieve with some of the liquor that has run through; this rather helps the process. Now soup made in this way, in which the head of celery, the onions, the carrots, the turnips, are all sent through the sieve, as well as the peas, is a very different affair from soup which has been simply flavoured by having them boiled in it. Indeed pea-soup should really be called purée of peas, and when pains is taken in its composition a very nice purée it is.

Pea-soup should, of course, be sent to table hot, and as it possesses, like all purées, the power of retaining its heat for some time, it is the better adapted for cold weather.

Some dried mint and some small pieces of toasted bread should always be sent to table with pea-soup; or small pieces of bread cut square, the shape of very small dice, may be fried a bright-golden colour in some hot lard. These pieces of bread, owing to their being crisper than toast, are better adapted for all sorts of purées, such as purée of Jerusalem artichokes or Palestine soup; the pieces of bread being dried after frying, on some blotting-paper.

With regard to the mint, take care to have it well sifted. If the mint is properly dried it will crumble easily on being pinched with the fingers, but the only way to avoid the stalks is to sift it. Mint can be bought ready dried in bottles in Covent-Garden Market, and at all good greengrocers'; and as a small sixpenny bottle will last a twelvemonth probably, and keep good almost for ever if well corked, it is advisable always to have a bottle in the house.

Another very excellent dish for cold weather is Irish stew. Irish stew has the following strong points in its favour as a dish for cold weather:—First it retains the heat for a long time; secondly, it contains a considerable amount of fat; and thirdly, which makes it a desirable dish for all weathers, is, it is probably the most economical dish ever sent to table. The best joint for making Irish stew is neck of mutton. First cut off nearly all the fat, the reason being that when mutton is boiled the fat swells enormously. The fat that is cut off will make an admirable suet pudding— another dish adapted for cold weather—that can be flavoured with grated lemon-peel. First pare about four pounds of potatoes, and cut them into slices, and allow them to boil for about a quarter of an hour; by this means the water contained in the potatoes will be extracted, and all water held in roots is far from wholesome. Next slice up five large onions, cutting them crossways, so that circular rings fall in slicing. Next take a good-sized stew-pan—an enamelled one is best—and cover the bottom with slices of potato and onions; add a little pepper and salt, and then cover this with a layer of meat, the quantity required being about three pounds. The trimmed neck or loin of mutton should be cut into rather thin chops, and the short bones at the end of the neck should, of course, be all cut into separate pieces. Again pepper and salt the meat, and cover it over with a thin layer of sliced potato and onion. The whole should be packed rather close—*i.e.* very little space should be left between the pieces, so that a very little water added will be sufficient to fill up the stew-pan, so that the top layer is moistened. Add this quantity of water, so as to avoid leaving any of the potato or onion uncovered. Next cover over the stew-pan, seeing that the lid fits close; place something heavy, such as a four-pound weight, on the lid to keep it down, and allow the whole to simmer gently for about three hours. Be careful, however, not to let it *boil*, as that is apt to render the meat hard. Also on no account take off the lid during the stewing process, as by so doing you let out the flavour.

It will be readily seen how exceedingly economical this dish is, as absolutely nothing is lost, as the liquor is eaten as well as the potato and onion. In roasting a joint some of the flavour necessarily goes up the chimney, and in boiling a joint some goes into the water in which the joint is boiled. Irish stew is, however, one of the few dishes in which there is absolutely no waste whatever.

One very seasonable, and at the same time delicious, sauce for winter is celery sauce; and in country houses where celery is grown in the garden, and can be had in abundance, a little should always be served with boiled turkey or boiled fowls.

First of all, cut up about six heads of celery and put them into boiling water, and allow them to boil for about ten minutes; strain them off, and throw them into cold water, and then drain and dry the pieces; next place them in a stew-pan, with about two ounces of butter and a little grated nutmeg, and allow them to dissolve slowly in the butter, but take care that the celery does not brown; when quite soft and tender, fill up the stew-pan with some good white stock that has been flavoured with some savoury herbs, such as marjoram, basil, and lemon-thyme; let the whole boil up, and then send it all through a wire sieve with a wooden spoon. Should the sauce not be thick enough, a little arrowroot may be added to it to thicken it; add also a little boiling milk, and a small lump of white sugar. Of course, when cream can be obtained it is far preferable to the milk. Another great advantage of having cream is that the sauce will look much whiter than when milk is used. The sauce may also be thickened with white roux—that is, butter and flour mixed together and baked, but not allowed to turn colour.

Celery sauce will be found to be by far the best accompaniment to a boiled turkey, which at the present season of the year seems to have that monopoly of one end of the table that the sirloin of beef seems to have of the other.

XVI.—CHRISTMAS DINNERS.

ONCE more the season has come round in which our Saviour's birth is celebrated, and though more than eighteen centuries have passed away, still the clarion voice rings as fresh as ever in our ears—" Goodwill toward men." From the highest to the lowest the sacred charm still works its magic spell. What child was ever sent to bed before its time, no matter what the crime, on Christmas Day? Oh, if we could only embed in our hearts throughout the year one half the charity that for very shame seems forced on us on this great festival, how far happier should we be!

It is not, however, now my province to dwell upon the sacred character of the day, yet the whole subject is so deep, so unfathomable, that, like a still phosphorescent sea, the slightest touch is instantly surrounded by a halo of glory, faintly and dimly revealing to finite minds the infinite brightness that is hidden in its breast, and I cannot bear to enter into the practical details of the day's festivities without some slight allusion in honour of the Author and Founder of the feast.

Now—the higher duties of the season being of

course left out of the question—Christmas Day without its dinner would be like the play of "Hamlet" with the part of Hamlet omitted. A genuine Christmas dinner, too, reveals our real national taste, and proves to ourselves and all the world that we have not yet acquired a French one. I wonder if it is possible for a statistician to calculate how many huge sirloins of beef and immense turkeys are consumed on Christmas Day. Such substantial fare—so unkickshawlike. Nor must we forget the goose of humbler life. Were it possible to calculate the exact amount of gratification given by mere eating, it would probably be found that the aristocratic sirloin and turkey fail to compare with the goose and sage and onion. We may add, especially the sage and onion.

We will suppose the happy morning to have arrived, and the children gathered round the table, with cheeks so flushed with pleasure and anticipation that they rival in colour the bright-red berries that glisten in the holly on the walls. Bright eyes to match the bright cheeks, eyes that have sparkled brighter as the well-known and looked-for chink has occurred, as the annual Christmas-box has been slipped into the hand by the grey-haired father or uncle, as the case may be—whose own eye is tinged with water as his mind goes back to the time, too, when he himself was a boy, without a care or thought of the morrow, and who, conscious of the joy he's giving, walks away with a lighter pocket but far lighter heart.

Happy, happy times! Is there one who at such a moment has an anxious care? Yes—suppose the beef should be raw, the mince-pie burnt, and the pudding all tumble to pieces the moment it is turned out. Were it known, I daresay tears have been shed upon such trifles; but then trifles make up life.

Perhaps the deepest anxiety is about the pudding. I will give the following recipe, which I have always found an excellent one. The ingredients required are—one pound and a half of muscatel raisins, half a pound of currants, quarter of a pound of sultana raisins, half a pound of mixed candied peel, three-quarters of a pound of bread-crumbs, three-quarters of a pound of suet chopped fine, nine eggs, quarter of an ounce of pounded bitter almonds, a table-spoonful of flour, a table-spoonful of moist sugar, and a quarter of a pint of brandy.

The first thing to do is to stone the raisins. Cut the raisins into two pieces, and in taking out the pips or stones be careful not to take out the pulp. For this reason it is undesirable to leave the stoning of the raisins to young persons. It is more than human nature can bear, and the strongest-minded child is apt to suck his or her fingers during the process, which, in addition to being far from nice, is apt to detract from the rich muscatel flavour of the pudding. The currants should be bought some days before they are wanted, in order that they may be first washed and then dried. Spread them out on a large sheet of coarse paper before the kitchen fire, and occasionally stir them about. They will also require picking, and this wants both care and patience; those little tiny stalks of the currants are very disagreeable to get into the mouth, and still more into a hollow tooth, for which they seem to have a natural affinity. The candied peel should be sliced into little, very thin slices, and not chopped up. The bread-crumbs should be made as fine as possible, and the suet chopped up very fine. Care should be taken to get the very best beef suet, that will chop properly, as some suet has a tendency to get into a creamy mass; when this is the case it is impossible to make a proper pudding of it. The dry ingredients should now be placed in a large basin, and thoroughly mixed together, care being taken to put in the pounded bitter almonds little by little. The eggs should be broken one by one into a cup, in order to see that each one is perfectly fresh. One stale egg will quite spoil a pudding. Beat up the eggs all together till they froth, and mix them in with the rest, and add the brandy. If the bread-crumbs were properly dried, it would not be found to be too moist.

Next take a new pudding-cloth, that has been well boiled in plain water, and butter it thoroughly, and then flour it. Turn the pudding into it and tie it, leaving room for the pudding to swell. The cloth must be fastened very securely, and it is as well to tie it in two places, in case of accidents. This pudding must now be boiled for at least six hours. It will always be found best to make the pudding some days before it is required; hang it up in the cloth, putting something underneath it to catch the drops; and a pudding made as we have directed will keep good for months and months. It only requires warming up for a couple of hours in a large saucepan of boiling water, and then turning out.

Now that awfully critical moment—turning out. Care should be taken to peel off the cloth, and not pull it; the reason of this is self-evident. On Christmas Day a piece of bright holly, with some red berries on it, should be stuck on the top of the pudding, and some lighted brandy poured over and round it. If you take my advice, you will light the brandy in the room.

To carry a large flat dish with ignited brandy is extremely dangerous, and I have not forgotten that dreadful story which appeared in the papers one or two years ago, about the poor girl who was burnt to death by the lighted brandy from the Christmas pudding falling on her white muslin dress.

In order to light the brandy, get a large iron spoon and fill it with brandy, get a lighted cedar taper or thin wood-shaving, or even a piece of paper rolled up, and act exactly as if you were going to boil the brandy in the spoon; in a few minutes the brandy will light of its own accord, when it can be poured on the pudding, and more added if required. If it is evening, and young children are present, it is as well to turn down the gas very low, or remove the candle for a few minutes. Judging by my own recollections, the lighted plum pudding was a great event in my early days—slightly awful, but intensely delightful.

With regard to the beef, I need say but a few words. It is a question between you and the butcher, and I will say butchers, as a rule, behave very well at Christmas-time, and while I think of it, I would recommend you to give your carving-knife to the butcher-boy, and tell him to get it well sharpened for the occasion, a hint that will not be forgotten—the day after Christmas will have its due effect. But sirloin of beef has a trying piece of gristle at the top, and without a sharp knife a very handsome piece will be made to look ragged. Have a good roaring fire. A piece about twelve pounds will take three hours. It will not require much basting, but remind the cook that it is the sides, and not the fat part, that should be basted. Some stupid women forget this. Let the dish for the beef be thoroughly hot; and this takes time. Have also some curly white horseradish to pile on the top of the joint, and be sure the dish-cover is hot, without being smoking.

We will next discuss the mincemeat, and would recommend a trial of the following recipe:—Take three apples, three lemons, one pound of raisins, three-quarters of a pound of currants, one pound of suet, quarter of a pound of raw beef, two pounds of moist sugar, four ounces of mixed candied peel, quarter of a rind of a fresh orange, one tea-spoonful of powdered mixed spice composed of equal proportions of cloves, cinnamon, and nutmeg; half a pint of brandy, and one glass of port wine.

Peel the apples and cut out the cores very carefully, and then bake the pieces till they are quite soft. Squeeze the lemons, and cut away the white pappy part, and boil the lemon-peel till it is fairly soft. The raisins must of course be carefully stoned, and the currants well washed and dried, and picked, as in the case of the pudding. Chop the suet very finely, as well as the raw meat and lemon-peel. Mix all the ingredients well together, and add the brandy last of all, and press the whole down into a stone jar, and place a piece of paper soaked in brandy on the top. Remove the paper and stir up the mixture thoroughly every three days, replacing the paper; if this is done, the mincemeat will keep good a long time.

To make the pies, roll out some thin puff-paste, butter a small round tin, and line it with a piece of paste, then place in a generous quantity of the mincemeat, and cover it over with a similar piece of puff-paste, and bake it in a moderate oven. Mince pies are none the worse for being warmed up, but pray take care that they are sent to table hot.

Let us next proceed to the goose. Now a fine, large, tender goose, with a sauce-tureen of fine rich gravy, and another of hot apple sauce, with a nice large floury potato, is not to be despised, and to my mind is worth half a dozen turkeys. I am afraid the sage and onion, the necessary accompaniment, causes it to be considered rather a vulgar dish. Never mind, let us be vulgar; it's only once a year. The principal thing is the stuffing. Onions vary so in size that it is a little difficult to describe, but for a large goose you must take five large onions and ten fresh sage-leaves. If you are obliged to put up with dried leaves, you will want nearly twice the number. Take rather more than a quarter of a pound of bread-crumbs, about a couple of ounces of butter, and add some black pepper and salt.

Chop the onions very fine with the sage-leaves, and mix all up together; and the yolks of a couple of eggs may be added if you wish to have the seasoning very rich, but they are by no means necessary.

This will make the stuffing that nine persons out of ten really prefer, but do not like to say so. If, therefore, you really wish to have the stuffing mild, the only difference must be, you must cut out the cores of the onions and partially boil them, and let them drain on a napkin; this takes away considerably the strong onion-flavour of which some persons are not very fond. Fill the goose with the stuffing, and roast it before a quick fire. Care must be taken that the goose is well tied up, to prevent the stuffing coming out at one end, or its getting filled with grease during basting at the other. A good-sized goose only requires one hour and a half to roast, and the general fault is that people will over-roast them, and dry them up. The largest goose I have ever seen would not take more than two hours, but try in the case of a very large one to have the stuffing off the chill before you put it in. Serve some rich brown gravy and apple sauce in a separate tureen, as you will be sure to splash the gravy in carving the goose if any is put on the dish.

With regard to roast turkey I can only say that no possible time can be given for roasting, as they vary so—especially in the present day of plump prize birds—that even the weight would be no criterion. A small turkey will require one hour and a half; while a very large one may want five hours. One word of caution about the stuffing. Every one knows how unpleasant a tendency what is called veal stuffing has to "rise." This is, I believe, owing to too much lemon-peel being almost invariably used. When you use a quarter of a pound of beef suet, a quarter of a lemon is amply sufficient. To this quantity may be added a couple of tea-spoonfuls of dried mixed stuffing-herbs (which can be bought in bottles at Covent Garden Market), two ounces of lean ham, rather more than a quarter of a pound of bread-crumbs, two eggs, a little chopped parsley (about a tea-spoonful or rather more), and a little grated nutmeg, salt, and cayenne pepper. Mince all the ingredients very finely together, and pound them afterwards in a mortar.

A very nice stuffing for turkeys can be made from chestnuts, but space will not allow me to enter into further details.

In conclusion, let me add, let Christmas come as a blessing, and not as a curse.

The demon Alcohol is abroad at this holy season, and many know that they require an archangel's strength to trample him underfoot. Let the law of each feast be regulated like that of the wise Eastern monarch: "None did compel." Let every one on Christmas Eve endeavour to find some case of distress which it is real and not false charity to alleviate. He will doubly enjoy his own dinner who can think that some one but for him would have gone without. It is such deeds that entitle us to say—

> ———— ———"That his bones,
> When he has run his course, and sleeps in blessings,
> May have a tomb of orphans' tears wept on 'em."

CHRISTMAS CHEER.

THERE is something sacred in the very name of *home* to every true-born Englishman, and, as we should naturally expect from the hallowing influence of this holy season of the year, home seems doubly sacred on Christmas Day. How many thousand families throughout the land are united but once a year! what efforts, too, do some make, so that on their great annual holiday they may once again find shelter under the old and loving parental wings!

But let us this year anticipate the day's festivities, and Christmas Eve finds us once again reunited round the fire, on which the log is heaped, and crackles brightly: for no one, unless by abject poverty compelled, would have a poor fire on Christmas Eve.

The fresh-cut holly glistens on the wall, the curtains are drawn, and the grey-haired, bright-eyed old man, as he glances round the circle, his voice too full almost to speak, yet feels an inner comfort difficult to describe—a feeling partly of thankfulness, partly of resignation, as he looks forward to the fast-approaching time when the places that know him now shall know him no more for ever. For it has been well said that children, though they increase the cares of life, yet mitigate the remembrance of death. But such a good old-fashioned circle round the fire on such a night would not be complete without a steaming bowl of something hot, to drink a toast in memory of yet another happy gathering in the old house at home. So, while the party assembled listen to the distant sound of the waits, or perhaps to the still preferable music of the bird of dawn—which recalls one of the brightest gems that have dropped from the pen of our greatest poet—we will, after repeating the lines, step down-stairs, and brew a bowl of bishop :—

> "Some say that ever, 'gainst that season comes
> Wherein our Saviour's birth is celebrated,
> This bird of dawning singeth all night long :
> And then, they say, no spirit dares stir abroad :
> The nights are wholesome ; then no planets strike,
> No fairy takes, nor witch hath power to charm,
> So hallowed and so gracious is the time."

Bishop, a good old-fashioned drink, whose nose has, so to speak, been somewhat put out of joint by mulled claret since that beverage has become so cheap, is best made as follows:—First take a small lemon, and at this season of the year they will be easily obtained white and new. First wash the lemon in a little warm water, and then stick into it a dozen or more cloves, and make the lemon hot by placing it in a plate in the oven, or better still, by suspending it from a string in front of the fire, taking care that the lemon does not hang too close, so as to get so hot as to split. Next take a little water, about a tumblerful, and pour it into an enamelled saucepan, and add to it a stick of cinnamon about six inches long—of course, breaking up the cinnamon; also put in the juice of a small lemon, one blade of mace, a quarter of a nutmeg grated, and four lumps of sugar that have been rubbed over the skin of a fresh pale-looking lemon. Put a lid on the saucepan, and let these spices boil on the fire gently for half an hour, or a little more. Next take a bottle of port wine, and decant it gently, in case of sediment, in the ordinary way; heat this in a saucepan, *but do not let it boil;* as soon as it is hot, pour the wine into a bowl previously made thoroughly hot with hot water, add the liquor of the spices and lemon-juice through a strainer, place the hot lemon in the bishop, and grate a little fresh nutmeg over the top, and add sufficient sugar to the whole, according to the tastes of the party. Of course, this is a somewhat strong mixture, and is certainly not altogether suited for children in any quantity. However, by adding more boiling water and more sugar it can soon be made weaker. Of course, the proper vessel into which the bishop should be poured is a punch-bowl. Unfortunately, punch-bowls are somewhat rare. If the party is tolerably large, a wash-hand basin makes a very fair substitute. Of course, you would pick a small one, and as ornamental as possible. Now, a thick basin requires a good deal of warming, so should you adopt my suggestion, recollect to fill the basin with boiling water some time before it is wanted. In lieu of a punch-ladle, the soup-ladle will be found a worthy substitute. I would also remind you of warming the glasses, not only for the sake of keeping the bishop hot, but to avoid breakages. In cold weather, especially when it is frosty, pouring any hot liquid into a cold glass is very apt to end in cracking it. The bowl too, should be placed in front of the fire on a hassock in the centre of the family circle.

Mulled claret is made in a very similar manner to bishop, only no roasted lemon is required. Take a small quantity of water, and boil in it for some time the same quantity of cinnamon and mace as recommended for the bishop, but do not put in any lemon-juice. After this has boiled for some time, add some white sugar—a dozen lumps or more, for claret requires a far greater amount of sugar than port. After adding the sugar, do not boil up the water and spices, as the addition of the sugar makes it extremely likely to boil over. Next warm a bottle of claret on the fire, taking care, as before, not to let it boil. When it is thoroughly hot, strain off the sweetened and spiced water, and add a little grated nutmeg, and a table-spoonful of pale brandy. If you have a large jug with a strainer in the spout, there is no occasion to strain off the spices. Mulled claret is generally put into a jug, and not into a bowl.

There is a good old-fashioned sound about the "wassail-bowl." I have never tried the following recipe, but will give it, as it sounds fairly correct:— Heat in a saucepan a pint of Burton ale, with half a pound of sugar, a grated nutmeg, and half an ounce f grated ginger; after it has just boiled up, add a quart more ale, four glasses of golden sherry, and a couple of ounces of lump sugar that has been rubbed over the outside of a lemon. Add also a few thin slices of lemon. Make the whole mixture hot without boiling it, and add half a dozen roasted apples that have had the cores stamped out and cut, but that have not been peeled.

Of course, this must be placed in a bowl, which

must be treated, as we said, with hot water. The sort of ale that must be used for the wassail-bowl is evidently strong old ale, like Burton or Edinburgh, and I should think the more sweet and oily the ale the better the wassail. Mild ale or bitter ale would not answer, especially the latter.

I have on previous occasions gone into the mysteries of mince pies and plum pudding, as well as into turkey-stuffing and goose-stuffing. How to roast a sirloin of beef, though important, is too well known to warrant many words. There is, however, no season in the year in which cold roast beef is so plentiful as the day after Christmas Day. Now, though cold roast beef really does not want any sauce at all, yet there is one that so admirably suits it that I think it is well worth mentioning at the present season. I refer to horseradish sauce. Horseradish sauce used to be made by mixing together grated horseradish with sugar, mustard, vinegar, and cream. There has, however, been an admirable modern invention called Swiss milk, preserved in tins. When, therefore, you have any compound requiring cream and sugar, by using Swiss milk with ordinary milk you get an exactly similar result, at a far less cost. To make horseradish sauce proceed as follows:—Take a stick or two of horseradish, and send it through a coarse grater till you have sufficient pulp to fill, say, a couple of tablespoons. This grating process, like chopping onions, is far from pleasant, as it makes one cry. Next dissolve about a tea-spoonful of Swiss milk in a little ordinary milk—say two table-spoonfuls of the latter—and mix in about a tea-spoonful of made mustard and a tea-spoonful of vinegar, then mix in the two table-spoonfuls of horseradish pulp, and stir it all together.

The consistency should be that of good thick cream; of course, by adding more pulp the mixture will be rendered thicker. Should it be too sweet, of course it is owing to there being too much Swiss milk, and as Swiss milk is apt to vary somewhat in sweetness, it is as well to act cautiously in using it, as it is always easy to add, but impossible to take away. Some persons, when serving horseradish with hot beef or hot rump steak, warm the sauce; this is a great mistake, as by warming the sauce you utterly spoil it, and to my mind render it absolutely disagreeable.

In speaking of Christmas dinners last year, I mentioned that an exceedingly nice stuffing for turkeys can be made from chestnuts. As anything in connection with turkeys is very *apropos* of the present season, I will describe how to make chestnut stuffing and chestnut sauce. For a large turkey, take about sixty chestnuts and slit the skins, and fry them for a short time in a little butter in a frying-pan till their husks come off easily. Then boil the chestnuts in some good strong stock till quite tender; take one-half and pound it in a mortar, with a little pepper and salt and scraped fat bacon; stuff a turkey with this and an equal quantity of ordinary veal stuffing or sausage-meat.

With regard to the sauce, take the remainder of the chestnuts and mix them with some good strong gravy, rubbing the whole through a wire sieve with a wooden spoon; a couple of lumps of sugar and a glass of sherry are an improvement. Of course, the best stuffing of all for turkeys is made from truffles, but then they are so expensive, as a rule, that the recipe would not be practical.

XVII.—TURTLE SOUP.

THERE can be no doubt but that the season of Christmas is especially associated with eating and drinking. The most approved English method of exhibiting "goodwill towards men," is by asking them to dinner. How many families there are with poor relations, in one respect resembling Christmas itself: they only come but once a year! The hallowing influence of this holy season may be seen in all classes. The haughty relax somewhat of their pride, and have what is called quite a family party—often the event of the year to the children of the above-mentioned poor relations. How much more of true enjoyment to the giver is there, however, in this dinner than in some of a different nature during the height of the season! So gracious and so hallowed is this time, that the miser relaxes, though reluctantly, his purse-strings; the workhouse-master approaches nearer to a man and a brother. The weary and heavy-laden prisoner is, in his fare, reminded once again of the outer world from which he is debarred. And even the hobnailed-booted ruffian refrains from kicking his wife on Christmas Day.

But the part of Christmas with which we are more especially concerned is the dinner-party. And our endeavour will be to help and advise that large class, the very backbone of English society, whose status may perhaps be best described by saying that they are blessed with neither poverty nor riches. To the really poor, the Christmas dinner is very dependent on the poor man's friend, the baker's oven. Early on the day the goose is carried there, prepared often in the somewhat primitive fashion of a heap of sage and onion on one side of the dish, and a pile of potatoes on the other. It is to be trusted that the baker's man is an honest one. A small piece cut off each joint of meat before baking, on Sunday, too often maintains the man for the week. The poor know to their cost how much meat will shrink in the baking. On Christmas Day the number of geese sent to each baker's is something extraordinary.

An ingenious baker once solved the following problem :—How to make a very small goose into a very large one. He purchased the smallest and cheapest that could be found, and substituted it for the smallest one sent to him to bake. By the simple method of making each person have the next smallest goose to the one he sent, the baker retained for himself the finest of the lot.

But we will now soar into the more aristocratic

region of mock-turtle soup and boiled codfish, roast sirloin of beef, boiled turkey and oyster sauce, plum pudding and mince pies. At least, we think we have heard of such dishes at this season of the year as being occasionally used.

However, one word of warning. The following awful catastrophe actually occurred: *Scene*—A dinner-party. *Time*—Soon after Christmas. *Host*—A nephew, with a wife and very large family. *Important Guest*—An uncle, rich—very rich; a bachelor; elderly, but irritable. At the moment the covers are taken off, he rises from the table, wrath written on his brow: "I will stand it no longer; give me my hat. This is the twelfth day running I have had roast beef and boiled turkey. I'll stand it no longer!" *Exit in a rage.*

Now, as I said in my last article, there is such a demand for mock-turtle soup about Christmas-time that calves' heads have been known to fetch a guinea apiece; but every housekeeper knows how exceedingly expensive they are at this season.

The change, however, of real turtle soup for mock is in the opinion of most people a change for the better, and we will fulfil the promise we made in another article, and describe as clearly as we can how to make real turtle soup from the dried turtle flesh, at a less cost than mock-turtle soup can be made from calves' head when the latter is very dear.

The first thing to be done is, of course, to purchase some of the dried flesh, which is generally about ten shillings a pound, and can be obtained from any of the large London provision-merchants—and is occasionally kept by the better-class grocers.

Now the general fault that we have found people express in regard to cookery-books, is that they invariably describe how to make such large quantities that the recipes are only adapted to hotels. It is evident, too, that if a cook can make three pints of soup, she could make three gallons. We will therefore describe how to make a small quantity of turtle soup—viz., three pints, which, by-the-by, is amply sufficient for ten people, or even more. Let those who doubt this—and they will be many—go at once, and see how many ladlefuls there are in a pint—the average is five. Now, at the commencement of a good dinner one ladleful is ample for each person. Three pints of soup would therefore give fifteen people one help each, but of course it would not do to have only just enough. Beau Brummel once said that he would never speak to a man again who came twice for soup; but he would be a brave man who would risk no one asking for more, when the party is a family one at Christmas-time, and the soup real turtle.

First, the turtle-flesh must be obtained at least three days before the soup is required. Suppose, then, a quarter of a pound to be in hand. It has somewhat the appearance of glue. Place it in a basin of cold water about the temperature of a hot summer's day, and let the basin, which had better be covered with a plate, be kept in a warm place, such as a top shelf in the kitchen. The very last thing before the cook leaves the kitchen for the night, or when the kitchen fire has got low, and will have no more coals put on it, is for the basin to be placed in the oven. This is especially necessary in winter. In the morning the basin must be taken out before the fire is lit, and the water changed—*i.e.*, the flesh, which will be found to be a little swollen, put into fresh cold water, and if it smells rather offensively—somewhat like high fish— there is no harm in rubbing it all over gently with a lump of salt. This soaking process had best be continued for three days and nights, at the end of which period the flesh will be, comparatively speaking, soft, especially the thinner pieces. The last twelve hours the water may be quite warm, but not hotter than that the cook's hand can be borne in it without inconvenience.

The turtle-flesh must be then cut up into small pieces about two inches square, and boiled for about twelve hours in some stock prepared as follows—and it is in the preparation of this stock that the real secret of making good turtle soup lies.

Now, turtle soup requires far stronger stock than is required for ordinary soup, and it should be borne in mind that it is always considered a great luxury, and when purchased ready-made the usual price is a guinea a quart. I have mentioned this, as I consider in the present day an apology is due for recommending the buying of gravy-beef for making soups for small families where economy is of the slightest moment. It is, as a rule, quite unnecessary.

But to proceed—we consider real turtle rather an exception to general rules :—

Take a pound and a half of gravy-beef, an equal quantity of knuckle of veal, and one slice of lean raw ham, and place them in a large saucepan, which we will suppose to be perfectly clean, lid as well. Place in also the following :—One head of celery, two onions—one of which has half a dozen cloves stuck in it—a small turnip and carrot, about as much parsley as would fill a tea-cup, two tea-spoonfuls of dried marjoram, two tea-spoonfuls of dried basil, half a tea-spoonful of lemon-thyme, and rather less than half a tea-spoonful of a herb called pennyroyal. All these herbs can be obtained at Covent-Garden Market in sixpenny and shilling bottles, the latter herb being sold by the bunch. Add a small tea-spoonful of salt and a *little* cayenne pepper, bearing in mind that these last commodities vary considerably in strength, and that it is always easy to add more, but impossible to take back. Fill the saucepan, which ought to be a gallon one, nearly full with cold water. Put it on the fire to simmer gently for at least twelve hours, occasionally skimming off any scum that may have risen. Unless the above has been placed on the fire early in the morning, it will be necessary to continue the operation of extracting the flavour and goodness from the meat, herbs, &c., the following day, in which case recollect that the whole must be turned out into a large basin at night, and covered over with a cloth. Inexperienced cooks would do well to bear in mind the following maxim :—*If soup be left in the saucepan all night, it will be utterly spoilt.*

When the above has simmered long enough, and has been reduced by this means to about two quarts, it must be carefully strained into a basin, and all the fat removed in the usual way. We would then recommend as follows, premising that it is not absolutely necessary, though a great improvement, mentioning this as in some parts of the country the ingredient could not be obtained.

Get, if possible, a couple of pounds of conger-eel, and boil it in the stock for an hour or more ; this had better be done where conger-eel is readily obtained, and cheap. Where, however, it is not, get for the previous day's lunch, or dinner, a pound or a pound and a half of the ordinary fresh eels; cut them into small pieces about two inches long, and let them boil gently in the stock till they are quite tender. Take them out with a strainer, throw them into a saucepan of boiling water for a minute, and then place them in a dish with enough boiling water to cover them, throwing in a couple of sprigs of fresh parsley. It is an exceedingly nice dish, often served at fish dinners, and called eel souchet. Brown bread and butter should be handed with it. By this means the soup gets a fish stock added to it, and there is no waste, as the fish is eaten. Of course the ordinary method of cooking the fish is to boil it in water. When this is done it will be found that the water in which the fish is boiled, when it is cold, becomes quite a jelly. Now all this glutinous substance helps the soup. The soup must be again carefully strained, and, if it is necessary, cleared with a couple of whites of eggs, and then run through a jelly-bag a few times in front of the fire. The soup must then be placed in an enamelled saucepan, and the turtle-flesh added to it and boiled till it is as tender as thoroughly-cooked calf's head; during this process of boiling, the soup will probably reduce itself to the desired quantity—viz., about three pints; to this must be then added a claret-glassful of madeira, which can now be obtained really good at forty shillings a dozen from any respectable wine-merchant. If, however, it is not thought necessary to have madeira bought on purpose—and it is a somewhat rare wine in the present day—a similar quantity of *good* golden sherry will do. The soup is now done, and only requires a few drops of lemon-juice added to it after it is put in the tureen.

One of the greatest mistakes in the use of wine for cooking is to think that *any* wine will do. I have known cases where people have ordered a few bottles of what they chose to call cooking sherry from the grocers, and filthy stuff it has been—enough to spoil anything. If you think turtle soup does not deserve a glass of good wine, my advice is, do not make any. It is no use adding a glass of some horrible concoction called sherry or madeira, and then tasting the soup and saying, "Ah! it is not a bit like what we had at Francatelli's." Of course it is not, and you have only yourselves to blame. The same thing applies to real mock-turtle. "What does he mean by *real* mock-turtle?" I can imagine you saying. But we live and learn. This is exactly the question I asked a waiter many years ago. We were discussing the important subject of what I should have for dinner.

"Soup, sir? yes, sir; very nice mock-turtle sir—real mock-turtle, sir."

This led to the disclosure—it was in the country—that it was made from calf's head, not pig's head.

Now, more than three-parts of the mock-turtle soup sold in London—I do not mean in the better-class hotels or restaurants—is made from pig's head, and very nice it is too. Were it really made from calf's head, it could not possibly be sold for the money. At some future period, when speaking on the all-important subject of "economy" in cooking, I will give you the recipe. Half a pig's head can be bought for nine-pence; nine persons out of ten would not tell the difference between soup made from it and soup made from calf's head. As the pieman said to Sam Weller, "It's the seasoning as does it."

In the above directions, I have only mentioned what I consider absolutely essential. When so many things are mentioned in recipes, people are apt to despair of trying them. However, there are several little things that might be added to the above stock during the period of making cooking with advantage: some chicken-bones, bearing in mind that they must have no white sauce in connection with them, or the soup will never be clear. A mushroom would be another little improvement; any odd scraps of meat, especially roast meat, may be added. The only difference between clear turtle and thick is that the latter has some brown thickening added to it. But it is, in my opinion, a great mistake to begin dinner with a thick soup, which is a capital thing to lunch off in cold weather, but it is apt to spoil the very best sauce—viz., appetite. The best recipe I know of for this sauce is exercise. Of course it is quite possible to have too much of a good thing, and this was the opinion of a certain gentleman, who once went out to dinner, as follows :—

He was a short, middle-aged gentleman, with a waistcoat that conveyed the idea of having swallowed a water-melon. He was not, as may be imagined, fond of exercise as a rule, and consequently took a cab to go out to dinner. Unfortunately, the cab was old and rotten, and the bottom gave way and came clean out, seat and all. The unlucky man inside had consequently to trot the whole way through the mud. As the cabman, quite unconscious of what had happened, drove on at a brisk pace, the middle-aged gentleman fruitlessly endeavouring to attract his attention all the time. On arriving at his destination, his feelings, as well as his legs, can be better imagined than described.

Cooking is a high art. There was some great foreign Minister, I forget who, who owed his great success as a diplomatist to his cook.

Suppose, for instance, some young man required a little assistance from his father. Who, in his senses, would broach the subject half an hour before dinner? No, send home a woodcock, and tell the cook to take great pains with it, and send it up unexpectedly. Tell the butler to get up a particular bottle, such as '34 port, or '48 Château Margaux, or a bottle of very old East India madeira. Wait till the old gentleman is about half-way through his bottle, and then approach him with respectful and affectionate confidence.

I have got another recipe for an old aunt, worth thousands. It is, as I say, worth thousands—*i.e.*, if the aunt be old, rich, and capable of making a will. Yes, I will tell, and in so doing probably make hundreds of fortunes for others, some of whom may perhaps some day recollect me. The recipe is as follows:—Make the tipsy-cake with brandy.

XVIII.—FISH DINNERS.

We have discussed the subject of wedding breakfasts, which are so similar to nice little suppers that we were unable, when so doing, to give many practical recipes; but we will endeavour to make amends on the present occasion, and will commence by blowing our own national trumpet, by maintaining that we English, in cooking fish, beat the French as completely as they beat us in the making of entrées. There is ofttimes a connection between wedding breakfasts and fish dinners.

It has often happened that a little party of four or more have taken a run down the river to Gravesend or North Woolwich; the fish dinner has been enjoyed, the discussion on "What are whitebait?" concluded in the usual manner—viz., that no one knows; the well-iced cup has washed down the devilled bait; the stroll on the balcony, the cigar, the water—perhaps the moon—the heavy shipping dropping slowly down the river, &c., have followed in due course.

But we cannot always be running down the river; but the happy little wife is suddenly seized with the following happy thought—"Suppose we have a fish dinner at home!" I will tell you how to do it, right away from the flounders souchet down to the devilled whitebait at the finish, and if you exercise a little judgment, I can assure you that it is by no means so expensive or extravagant an affair as many think.

It must however, be carefully borne in mind that the one secret of success in the management of a little dinner consisting of a variety of dishes is—forethought. The cook should consequently divide the dinner into two distinct classes—viz., those dishes which can be cooked beforehand—*i.e.*, in the morning of the day—and those which require cooking at the last moment. To illustrate what I mean, I would mention stewed eels and whitebait. It is obvious that the first can be prepared hours beforehand, and will simply require warming up, but that the latter cannot be cooked till within a minute of its being sent to table.

I will now give a list of fish from which the fish dinner can be chosen, but at the same time would strongly recommend, where it is possible, some common-sense person to go early in the morning to Billingsgate Market, and pick out, say, half a dozen different kinds of fish, of course choosing those that are in season, and consequently cheapest: flounders, souchet and fried; eels, souchet, fried, and stewed; salmon, plain boiled and with piccalilly sauce; red mullet, *en papillote;* soles, filleted and fried; whiting;

turbot, boiled; smelts; lobster cutlets; whitebait, ordinary and devilled; shrimps, curried.

Of course I do not mean that you are to have all these fish at once, but as under ordinary circumstances it is almost impossible to get just what fish you may ask for, I give a variety, so that if one is not to be obtained, you may have some others to fall back upon. I would, however, at starting, remind you that *the* dish in a fish dinner is the whitebait.

We will first start in the dining-room, and suppose the time to be the hour of dinner. The table is laid for four; a green glass is placed, in addition to an ordinary sherry one, by the right-hand side of each person. The sherry is tapped, and let us trust it is dry, and free from fire, as sweet sherry is quite out of the question at a fish dinner. We will also suppose a bottle of chablis or sauterne to be on the sideboard, with a corkscrew run into the cork, ready for drawing. On the sideboard, also, are two plates, containing plenty of thin brown bread and butter, with not too much butter on the bread, and that, too, really fresh, without a turnipy flavour.

If you possess that comfort, fish-knives, all the better, but dessert-knives do very well as a substitute. We will suppose, then, two silver forks placed to each person, and the remainder of the silver forks on the sideboard ready for use, for recollect a series of fishes will soon exhaust even a large establishment of forks. Have ready, therefore, outside the door, a large jug containing hot water and soda, and a jug of ordinary water by its side. As the forks are taken out of the room, wipe them on a cloth, plunge them into the hot soda and water, and then into the ordinary water, wipe them on a clean cloth, and they are ready again for use. Half a dozen forks or more can be washed this way in half a minute.

We will next descend to the kitchen, and we there find everything neatly arranged. In the sink is already placed a large tub of boiling water and soda, and by its side another tub or basin of cold water. You will probably run short of plates, and certainly will of vegetable-dishes, and consequently I would recommend you, if possible, to borrow of a friend a couple of these latter dishes. In front of the fire, or on the hot-plate, is a pile of hot plates.

The stewed eels are in a small stew-pan on the side of the fire; the salmon and pickle sauce, in another stew-pan, ready; the curry sauce is likewise ready, say in a little egg-saucepan, and a small basin on the dresser contains the shrimps ready picked. The red mullet, *en papillote*, is ready in the tin in the oven, and the lobster cutlets are also ready arranged to be what the cook calls "popped in the oven" at the proper moment. But before going any further I will run as briefly as possible through the methods of preparing these dishes, some of which have been described before, but may have been forgotten. First, the stewed eels. Some good stock has been placed on the fire early in the morning, and into it have been put some button mushrooms out of a tin, and if possible a few very small spring onions; the stock has been thickened with some brown thickening—*i.e.*, butter and flour fried a brown-colour; to this have been added about a dessert-spoonful of mushroom ketchup and another dessert-spoonful of port wine, and a little cayenne pepper. The eels have been cut into pieces about two inches long, and placed in this and allowed to simmer slowly for an hour, or longer; the cook has then taken each piece of eel out very carefully, so as not to break them, and allowed the stock to boil up and settle; this has been skimmed once or twice, for a good deal of fat, or what looks like it, will be found on the top. The eels have then been put back in the stew-pan, and the whole allowed to simmer until the eels are as soft as possible, when the dish is finished, care being taken not to break the pieces when turned out. Next, the salmon and pickle sauce. This can be made from fish left the day before. Cut the cold salmon into pieces about three or four inches long and one and a half inches square, and simply warm these pieces up in some good strong brown gravy to which has been added about half a tea-spoonful of Worcester sauce, and about half a tea-cupful of mixed hot pickles in which cucumber, as indeed it generally does, slightly preponderates; take also care to have three or four chillies with it. Have the gravy a dark colour and well thickened, so that the pieces of salmon may be covered with it; a little arrowroot mixed with cold water may be added to the sauce in order to obtain the necessary thickness.

Next, the curry sauce in the little saucepan. This may have been, and should be, made long before; some curried mutton the day before for dinner will be found an advisable dish, as the sauce left will do for the shrimps, and a very little is necessary. Curry sauce is made by frying say six large onions in a stew-pan with butter till they are browned; three large apples added, and dissolved in it, some brown gravy, the whole thing rubbed through a tanning or sieve, taking care that all the onion *is* rubbed through; then a table-spoonful of curry paste and a dessert-spoonful of curry-powder added, and the whole thickened with brown thickening to its proper consistency. Have ready, hot, about half a tea-cupful of this sauce, add to it about half a salt-spoonful of anchovy sauce, put the shrimps in it for one minute only, turn them out, and serve some plain boiled rice with them on a separate plate.

Next, the red mullet. First take a piece of white foolscap paper, and oil it all over, next chop up a tea-spoonful of capers fine, next cut up into slices about three ounces of butter, lay the slices on the paper, sprinkle half the chopped capers on it, pepper and salt it, and lay the mullet on the butter, on its side, put the rest of the butter on the top with the capers and a little more pepper and salt, fold the paper over, and fold the edges over and over, so as to make the foolscap sheet of paper into the shape of those old-fashioned apple turnovers—a fat semi-circle; put this into a tin greased at the bottom to prevent the paper sticking, and put it in the oven. A small mullet will bake in half an hour; a very large one, nearly an hour. Send the fish up to table in its paper. If the butter or some of it has run out into the tin, pour it into the dish on which you place the paper.

Next, the lobster cutlets. These have, of course, been prepared before, and only require making hot in the oven. A lobster has been bought containing coral, which coral has been pounded in a mortar with about the same quantity of butter, and a pinch of cayenne, and some of this has been added to the meat of the lobster, pounded in a mortar with some more butter and some very finely-chopped onion and parsley, a piece of the former about as big as the top of the thumb, and a tea-spoonful of the latter, being the proper quantities; a little ordinary pepper and a teaspoonful of anchovy sauce have been added, and the mass shaped into little pats about as large as oval picnic biscuits; these have been egged over and covered with very fine bread-crumbs, then fried in hot fat for about a couple of minutes, and a little piece of red claw stuck into each at the finish by way of garnish.

Now these five nice dishes are all ready, and we presume the dishes have also been got ready to put them in. First of all we will take flounders souchet. Pick out the smallest flounders you can, boil them in some water with a little salt, when tender take them out with a slice, keeping the white side uppermost, and place them in a vegetable-dish of boiling water, drop into this water two or three little sprigs of clean double parsley, and serve quickly, handing round the brown bread and butter. Eel souchet can be done in exactly a similar manner. The cook must now have ready two frying-pans, one filled with hot boiling fat, and the other with fresh lard for the whitebait, to which we shall come by and by. We shall now suppose the fish for frying ready on a dish on the dresser, and we will take eels, filleted sole, flounders, whitings, smelts, &c.; now these must be all treated alike, first they must be dried, then floured, then dipped in well-beaten-up egg, then dipped in *fine dry* bread-crumbs, and then sprinkled over with fine bright golden bread-raspings, in order to insure the colour being right. Suppose the cook has just sent up the flounders souchet; let the next course be fried eels, and salmon and pickle sauce. Take the eels ready prepared and throw them into the boiling fat; if the fat boil, four or five minutes is ample time, if the fat is deep enough to cover the fish. Take a hot vegetable-dish, turn out the salmon and sauce into it, and put on the cover; next take a clean napkin and warm it, and fold it up, and put it on a hot dish; hold a dish-cover to the fire for a minute, and cover over the napkin; take the eels out of the fat and put them for half a minute on to a hot coarse cloth to drain, put them on the clean napkin with a few pieces of green parsley round, and send them up with the salmon. Suppose the next course is turbot, smelts, and red mullet; the turbot, or rather a slice of one, is supposed to be boiling in a saucepan; take it out and put it on a cloth to drain; take first half a dozen smelts and pop them into the fat you have just taken the eels out of; a very short time will cook them. Place the turbot on a fish-napkin, put a piece of parsley on the top of it, and place the fried smelts round the edge. The red mullet simply wants slipping off the tin on to an ordinary dish just as it is, and the next course is done. The lobster cutlets might be sent up with some fried fish instead, as we presume no one would think of having all this fish at one dinner.

We therefore now come to the whitebait, and will attempt to describe the secret of having this really delicious and delicate fish well cooked. Of course, in the first place, it is absolutely indispensable to have the fish perfectly fresh, and in an unbroken state, and it is on this account that whitebait is always had in the greatest perfection at the various hotels which overlook the river where the whitebait is caught. We will suppose, therefore, the whitebait is ready. Now everything depends upon expedition. The whitebait must be first dried and then plunged as speedily as possible into boiling fat. First we will suppose ready on the fire a deep frying-pan full of *boiling* lard; in order to insure the lard being sufficiently hot, let a drop of water fall into it and see if it hisses; next have ready a wire whitebait-basket, then throw the whitebait into some fine dry flour on a cloth; don't be afraid of having too much flour, as in these water-side hotels the flour is an inch thick; next shake the whitebait free of the flour in a wide sieve, something like what is used for sifting oats; this is for the purpose of getting rid as much as possible of the flour, to avoid the whitebait being pasty and clammy. Next, having put this floured whitebait into the wire basket, plunge it into the boiling fat—one minute will more than suffice to cook it—throw it on to a hot cloth for a few seconds to drain, and serve it *very* quickly. Whitebait sent to table properly should burn the mouth with fire-heat. Do not try and cook too many at a time, as they are liable to stick together. Also shake the wire basket a little in cooking them, for the purpose of avoiding this sticking-process; and when they are thrown on to the cloth, if you see one or two sticking together, separate them. Properly cooked whitebait should be crisp, but at the same time slightly soft in the middle, when eaten. There are two kinds of devilled whitebait—black devil and red devil; the former consisting of adding black pepper in the middle of cooking; and the latter, black and cayenne mixed. Have the pepper, whichever is fancied, ready in a pepper-box, lift the whitebait-basket out of the boiling fat, shake it and pepper the whitebait at the same time, put the basket back into the fat for a few seconds, and then turn the whitebait out on to the cloth. It will be found best to send up the whitebait in two dishes, first the ordinary, second the devilled; thin brown bread and butter should be handed round with it, besides some lemon cut into quarters.

It will sometimes be found that with whitebait are mixed a few shrimps or very small eels; these should properly be removed before sending to table, as they have the effect of destroying the appearance.

It may perhaps seem superfluous to add, that whitebait requires no sauce, yet the following conversation actually occurred at North Woolwich, where whitebait are caught and cooked in the greatest perfection:—

Visitor.—" Waiter, these whitebait are not so nice as they were last time."

Waiter.—" Perhaps, ma'am, you would like them better if you did not take anchovy sauce."

On one occasion some persons demanded melted butter with their whitebait. Whitebait in perfection should be small, but near the end of the season are, of course, far larger and by no means so delicate as in early spring. Waiters are proverbial for presence of mind, and on one occasion, when the whitebait was brought up, about the size of sprats, quietly answered the intended complaint of " Waiter, these whitebait are very large," by saying—" Yes, sir—very fine, sir."

The curried shrimps are generally served last of all, and then some meat—generally a roast fowl or duck—but, as a rule, no one eats much of this after all this fish. In a private house it would be better to have a little cold roast beef and salad to finish up with, as in ordinary kitchens a roast duck or fowl would be terribly in the way during cooking the dinner.

XIX.—WEDDING BREAKFASTS.

My chapter on wedding breakfasts must not consist in simply saying, Don't have one; though I must in the name of common sense enter my protest against the vulgarity—for it is nothing else—of giving one out of proportion to the means of the giver. Where money is no object, of course the simplest plan is to go to some first-rate confectioner's, and let them supply the breakfast at so much a head. Where, however, economy is a necessity, much can be done with a little good management to avoid waste. I will give an instance of a wedding breakfast that took place during the last six months, and the cost. For it often happens that during the last week before the wedding there is so much to be done at home in the trousseau line that any elaborate cooking in the house is almost impossible. The following bill of fare is one supplied for over sixty persons, at 14s. a head, in February last :—

POTAGES.
Printanier.
Purée d'Artichauts à la Palestine.

ENTRÉES CHAUDES.
Chartreuse de Homard à la Cardinal.

Petites Timbales à la Grande Duchesse.
Quenelle de Volaille à la Sefton.
Côtelettes de Tortue.

Saumon à la Mayonnaise.
Dindon aux Truffes.
Gelantine de Veau à la Jardiniere.
Langues de Bœuf.
Pâtés de Faisans à la Francaise.
Jambon, braisé.   Poulets rôtis.
Faisans rôtis.
Anguilles en Gelée â l'Aspic.
Petits Pâtés aux Huitres.
Pâté de Foie-gras en Aspic.
Mayonnaise de Filets de Soles.
Salades de Homard.

Gâteaux de Fruit à la Richelieu.
Fauchonette à la Prince de Galle.
Macédoine d'Abricots.
Gelées de Citron.   Gelées de Marasquin.
Crêmes d'Ananas.
Petits Choux à la Madère.
Chartreuse d'Orange à la Tangier.
Gelée à la Dauphine.
Meringue à la Suisse.
Petites Patisseries à la Bonne-bouche.
Meringues à Crême à la Curaçoa.
Fruit, &c. &c.
Glacés.
Boudins à la Princesse Alice Maude.

Now a breakfast like this, including as it does two soups and four hot entrées, cannot as a rule be done in a private house. This of course does not include wine; and when the breakfast is ordered from a pastrycook's, I would always recommend the wine to be supplied from the home cellar. A first-class cold breakfast from a good pastrycook's, with soup and ices, will cost about 12s. 6d. a head; and unless the weather be really very hot, soup is always desirable. Without soup and ices, a saving of about 1s. a head can be made.

There are many persons, however, who cannot afford even so much as 10s. a head for a breakfast from the pastrycook's. When, therefore, the breakfast is made at home, it had better be all cold except the soup; and the great secret of success will be found to be in the old adage—"Never put off till the morrow what can be done to-day." Have plenty of flowers, and if summer-time, have plenty of ice. Were I to go through a set of dishes, I should simply be repeating what I have already said under the heading of "How to Give a Nice Little Supper." Fruit, flowers, and ice make the greatest and best show possible for the money. Then, too, a few dishes can be bought which are not easily made at home. Some of those Italian shops where they sell ices have excellent meringues very cheap.

Perhaps the greatest sacrifice of all to that monster, Custom, is the wedding-cake. I suppose there never will be a case of a couple sufficiently strong-minded to forego themselves this luxury, on the ground of "what *would* people say?" Unless the cake required be very large, it is by no means a difficult thing to make at home, and it can be sent to be baked at the baker's, who will probably know it only requires a moderate heat, and that the oven should be kept at an even temperature all through the baking-process.

Take first of all some candied peel, orange, lemon, and citron, $\frac{1}{2}$lb. of each, and cut them into small, thin shreds; $1\frac{1}{2}$lb. of flour; $1\frac{1}{2}$lb. of butter; 1lb. of dried cherries, which should be cut up, but not too fine; $1\frac{1}{2}$lb. of currants, which must be thoroughly washed, picked, and afterwards dried; 8oz. of almonds, well pounded; eight eggs; the rind of four oranges rubbed on to sugar; $\frac{1}{2}$oz. of spices, consisting of ground cinnamon, nutmegs, and cloves in equal proportions; about a tea-spoonful of salt, and half a pint of good brandy. The butter should be well worked with a wooden spoon in a large, strong basin, till it has a sort of creamy appearance. The flour, eggs, and sugar should be added slowly, while the spoon must be kept working the whole time. After this has been thoroughly well mixed, the rest of the ingredients mentioned may be added, only a little at a time, to insure the whole quantity being properly mixed up. When this is done, it should be poured into a tin hoop, placed on a metal baking-sheet. Two sheets of well-buttered paper must be placed on the baking-sheet underneath, and the hoop itself must be lined with a double band of well-buttered paper, or else the cake will be sure to burn round the edges.

The cake may now be taken off to the baker's oven, and as it will keep good for a long time, and in fact improve in flavour by keeping, it should be made some time beforehand. The icing of the cake should not be done till a short time beforehand, as it of course has a tendency to get dirty.

First the almond part—the only part of a wedding cake, to my mind, worth eating.

Take ½lb. of almonds, and having skinned them by throwing them into boiling water, rubbing off the skins and then throwing them into cold water in order that they may not lose their colour, pound them very thoroughly in a mortar with 1lb. of the finest white sugar, add a very little orange-water, and sufficient white of eggs to make it all into a soft paste; but take care not to fall into the common fault of making the paste too soft. This paste may now be spread over the *top* of the cake, taking care to avoid its getting over the edge as much as possible, and the cake must be placed in a dry place. When the paste is sufficiently hard, the whole may then be iced over with sugar as follows:—Take six whites of eggs, and add to them about 1½lb. of very finely sifted, powdered white sugar. The whitest sugar must be chosen for the purpose. This must be worked well together with a wooden spoon, and a very little lemon-juice now and then dropped in while it is being worked. The mixture should properly have a shiny appearance, and if it is not thick enough it only requires a little more powdered sugar. This must now be put all over the cake to about a quarter of an inch in thickness. Some little skill will be necessary in order to avoid unseemly ridges in the icing on the top of the cake, which when covered must be put in a warm place in order to allow the icing to dry; only be sure to put a piece of paper as soon as possible lightly over the top, as should the dust settle while it is drying, the cake will not have that snow-white appearance it should have.

Little knobs of icing may be arranged round the edge to make the cake more ornamental, and on the day of the wedding a simple wreath of white flowers and green leaves will be found quite sufficient an ornament; in fact, a plain wreath of orange-blossoms, when it can be obtained, looks far better than any more elaborate attempt at ornament.

A wedding-cake is an expensive thing to make at

home, but a far more expensive thing to buy. For a highly-ornamented wedding-cake almost fabulous prices are asked; and there is something very satisfactory in having it made at home. A little ingenuity will easily enable any one whose fingers are gifted to make a small round centre ornament with glazed white cardboard, a little silver paper, and orange-blossom. When the cake is large, something raised in the centre is a great set-off to its appearance.

I trust what I have written may be the means of enabling some young couples to start in the world with some extra £20 or £30 in pocket than otherwise; but it is not so much to them that I would speak as to the conscience of the old boy, the bride's father, that I would address my remarks. You know you are really a little proud of what you think is getting your daughter off your hands respectably. You know, too, that you have never opened so many bottles of champagne in all your life before. You know, too, that many members of your son-in-law's family will visit you house on this occasion, that will probably never visit it again. Now has that fact anything to do with all this outlay, which you know you can't afford? Very likely: but then it is really very snobbish. No, paterfamilias, don't show off, and no one will think a whit the worse of you for it. Pocket your £50, give quite a plain breakfast—no champagne at all—brave the world, and then furnish a room in the new house with the money, and instead of calling it "the breakfast-room," call it "the wedding-breakfast room." One word in conclusion. If you *will* give champagne, give it good, or they will all laugh at you—they will indeed, they will laugh. Young men, bachelor friends of your son-in-law, will say, "Did you taste that fellow's wine? Wasn't it awful?"—which will call forth the remark, "Ah, I don't suppose he had opened many before." Therefore, whatever you do, give good champagne, or none.

XX.—FOOD FOR INVALIDS.

THE sick-room—what echoes does not the very name awaken in the memories of the past! There are few moments in our lives' history more solemn than those when we have watched by the bedside of one we love, whose life is trembling in the balance, and whose soul and body seem held together by so slight a thread that a breath of wind would part them. What vows have we not vowed, what good resolutions have we not formed, and how chastened have our minds been in these our hours of agony! for of very truth "adversity doth best discover virtue."

Then—the doctor's visit. With what an anxious look will the wife, wearied with watching, try and read his eyes as he feels the pulse of the languid patient! what a rush of joy fills her heart, as she sees the doctor smile! for hope is brightest when it dawns from fears. The crisis is past, the patient is pronounced much better, and is ordered some good strong beef-tea. With burning eyes and bursting heart the thankful wife turns away to give the necessary orders, not forgetful, let us trust, of her vows vowed, of her resolutions made, or of the Great Physician who alone can cause the blind to see and the lame to walk.

Like a calm sea to the tempest-tost, like a draught of water after parching thirst, like a bed of down to the wearied traveller, do these sweet hours of convalescence follow after those weary ones of watching, when hope deferred made the heart sick—

"Oh! these were hours, when thrilling joy repaid
A long, long course of darkness, doubts, and fears."

What pleasure, too, to watch the patient take his first cup of beef-tea or his first chop with evident enjoyment, and to see the faint tinge of colour return to the pale cheeks, foretelling of returning health and strength, as surely as the first blush of dawn upon the eastern mountain-tops foretells the coming day!

Again, too, the refreshment taken, the first long sound sleep, nature's great restorer, how different to watch now, to when the restless patient tossed and turned and muttered, and seemed to suffer more than when awake! There is something very beautiful in a calm and tranquil sleep—

"An infant when it gazes on the light,
A child the moment when it drains the breast,
  *   *   *   *   *
Feel rapture, but not such true joy are reaping
As they who watch o'er what they love while sleeping."

> "For there it lies, so tranquil, so beloved,
>   All that it hath of life with us is living,
>   So gentle, stirless, helpless, and unmoved,
>   And all unconscious of the joy 'tis giving."

But let us leave the convalescent chamber with the watcher and the watched, and descend to the kitchen, and see what we there can do to help on the recovery so happily going on above.

First let us take that probably most valuable of all invalids' preparations—viz., beef-tea. The quickest and best method of preparing good beef-tea is as follows:—Take a pound of good lean gravy-beef, cut it up into little pieces, pour over them a pint of *cold* water, and add a little salt. Then take a fork and squeeze these pieces in every direction, in order, as much as possible, to extract the juices out of the pieces of meat. Next place it all—*i.e.*, water and meat—in an enamelled saucepan, and place it by the *side* of the fire, not on the fire, and gradually heat it, taking the greatest care that it does not boil. Having continued this process for about an hour and a half or two hours, during the last half-hour keeping the beef-tea hot without boiling, strain the whole off through a strainer, pressing the meat again with a spoon, so as to squeeze as much as possible all the goodness out of it.

Then remove all the fat. This can be done by carefully skimming it, or, if time will allow, by letting it get cold, when the fat will harden on the top. Now, to my mind good beef-tea is one of the nicest things we can take when ill, but sick persons often tire of it, and loathe it. When this is the case, very often by adding a little sherry, and allowing it to get cold—when, if properly made, it will be a jelly—patients will take it in this form when they could not in the liquid state.

Veal broth and mutton broth are made on exactly the same principles as beef-tea, of course substituting either veal or mutton for the beef, and taking equal care to remove all the fat, and not to let the liquor boil.

Another method of making beef-tea very simply, in a way in which no careful watching is required, is to cut up a pound of gravy-beef as before, and simply put it with a pint of water into a stone jar, and put the jar in the oven; if the oven is not too hot—*i.e.*, not hot enough to absolutely make the liquid boil in the jar—this way will be found to be very good. Or the jar may be tied over with a cloth, and placed in a large saucepan of boiling water on the fire, the water in the saucepan to be kept gently simmering.

Very often young children, and even babies, are ordered beef-tea. Now all mothers know the difficulty at times of inducing sick children to take anything, and beef-tea by no means recommends itself to a child's appetite. Forcing food down a child's throat against its will should never be resorted to, save as a last resource, and at the doctor's order. There are many means, however, by which little children can be persuaded to take things, which sensible mothers probably know of. In the case of beef-tea an admirable plan is, instead of using salt, use a little sugar, and make the beef-tea sweet. Grown-up person would probably consider such a mixture nasty to a degree; not so, however, the child. Young children have a natural taste for sweet things, and a natural dislike to salt.

In very early life the food that nature has supplied for children is sweet. Salt, on the other hand, is decidedly an acquired taste. Our dear old friend Robinson Crusoe had considerable difficulty in inducing his man Friday to eat salt; and when he did, it was only in very small quantities.

The next dish of importance for consideration is arrowroot. First I would strongly recommend the Bermuda arrowroot, and not the St. Vincent; the latter is cheaper, but very inferior in quality. Bad arrowroot is absolutely unwholesome, and a good deal of the bad arrowroot—too bad, in fact, to be sold as arrowroot at all—is, I fear, used to mix with and adulterate corn-flour.

The first point to ascertain is whether the patient will take the arrowroot thick or thin; some persons have strong prejudices on this point, and thick arrowroot will require double the quantity of thin. Arrowroot is also made with water and milk, but the method is the same for both. Take a spoonful or two of cold water or milk, as the case may be, and mix in the powdered arrowroot in the cup or basin, and stir it up thoroughly; then pour the boiling water or milk slowly on to it, keeping it stirred the whole time. A little sugar may be added, and of course, when allowable, a little wine or brandy is a great improvement. When made with milk, a little grated nutmeg on the top also vastly improves the compound both in flavour and appearance.

A great deal of the prepared cocoa sold is simply cocoa and arrowroot mixed, consequently when the boiling water is poured on, the arrowroot causes the cocoa to look thick and nourishing. If you want to make a good cup of chocolate out of cake chocolate, all you have to do is to mix a little arrowroot in the cup with it, and the result will be that the chocolate will appear to be ten times as strong as it would otherwise do.

With regard to chicken broth, that fashionable invalid's preparation many years ago, we ought to say a few words, and these few will be unfavourable. There is, comparatively speaking, but little nourishment in it. In any case, however, should you make any, bear in mind that it is the bones, and not the flesh, that make the broth; so instead of wasting the whole fowl over the broth, cut off the meat, which can be made into nice rissoles or mince, and use the bones only for the broth.

Now minced mutton or chicken is often recommended for invalids, as being easily digested; but pray remember that invalid mince is very different from the ordinary mince of every-day life. In the first place, we all know that in ninety-nine cases out of a hundred mince is made from meat that has been cooked before. Now mince so made, though very nice and wholesome for persons and children in ordinary health, yet is by no means so easy of digestion —*i.e.*, the remains of a leg of mutton minced the second day would be less digestible than the cut off the joint on the first day, the warming-up process having naturally a tendency to harden the meat.

To make nice mince for an invalid, the meat must be minced raw. It must then be sprinkled with a little salt, moistened with a little good broth, and warmed slowly with the greatest care, as, should the broth boil for one second, the mince will be rendered tough and indigestible. It is obvious that mince made this way differs enormously from the ordinary mince. A very few minutes is sufficient, if the meat has been minced fine, to cook it—in fact, as soon as it is hot it is done.

Mince made in this manner is exceedingly nutritious, and it will often be found that weak digestions can take this when they can take nothing else.

Our two next preparations will be barley-water and toast-and-water. Two very simple things, it will probably be thought, and very unnecessary to describe. I will describe them, however, first as they generally are, and next as they ought to be.

How very often do you find the barley-water dirty! For instance, when you drink it out of a tumbler, you come to some black-looking stuff at the bottom. Again, how often do you find the toast-and-water thick, instead of bright! and far less appetising is it when it is so. Now both these defects arise from thoughtlessness or want of care.

First, then, barley-water. Take a couple of ounces of pearl barley and wash it thoroughly, and then place it in some boiling water, and boil it for about ten minutes. This has the effect of dissolving the outside of the barley. Strain it off, and put it into a couple of quarts of fresh boiling water, and let it boil gently till it has nearly half boiled away. Then strain it off, and flavour it with a little sugar and lemon-juice, putting in a small piece of peel. Barley-water is often made too thick. Patients, especially feverish ones, want something to drink. By adding water to it, it can, of course, be made as thin as wished. Barley-water should be kept in a jug, with a spoon in it, and stirred up each time before it is poured out, and only the quantity required poured out, as it settles and does not look nice—milky at the bottom and watery at the top.

Next, toast-and-water. First, "how not to do it." You will find a servant generally cut off a knobby piece of crust, stick a toasting-fork in it, and toast it very black, put this in a jug, and pour boiling water over it, and this great hunk of bread will be floating at the top. This toast-and-water will be poor, muddy-looking, and have a slightly floury taste. The proper method is to cut the bread *thin*, and toast both sides *thoroughly*, and also have plenty of it. Let the bread be toasted through—*i.e.*, let the bread be toasted so as to be thoroughly dried up. Then pour the boiling water on it, and, if liked, add a small piece of lemon-peel. Let this be carefully drained off, so that no crumbs remain in the fluid after it has got cold; and this toast-and-water, which will look bright like sherry, will be a welcome draught to the feverish invalid.

To make bread-and-milk, you must cut the bread up into small square pieces, and pour boiling milk on them. There are a good many persons who don't fancy bread-and-milk, who yet will take toast-and-milk. For this purpose you must pour the boiling milk over small pieces of toast similar to those that would be handed round with pea-soup.

In making bread-and-milk for infants, it is generally recommended to pour boiling water on the bread, and then drain it off, and then add the milk, as the boiling water renders the bread softer; and as medical men generally recommend a little water to be mixed with the milk for very young children, it will not be weaker. It is not for me to put up my opinion against the medical profession, but in London I would recommend mothers to give their children the milk pure when they have to buy it. I fear that many of the cows that supply London have iron tails, and that the doctors' recommendation has been already fully carried out—if anything, probably too fully.

Another very refreshing drink for invalids, especially in hot weather, is lemonade. This is too often made by simply squeezing a lemon into a tumbler, picking the pips out with a spoon, and then adding sugar and cold water. The best method of making lemonade is to peel the lemons, or otherwise the lemonade will be bitter; cut them into slices, taking away the pips, and then pouring boiling water on the slices, adding, of course, sufficient sugar to sweeten. This, after being well stirred, and the pulp pressed with a spoon, must be carefully strained through a piece of fine muslin, and allowed to get cold. When cold, a piece of ice is a great improvement. Cold, weak lemonade made this way, not too sweet, is one of the most refreshing drinks for hot weather possible; and in cases where there is a tendency to take fluids too often, a tendency, we fear, rather of the age in which we live, a large jug of lemonade, made in the manner we have described, will often prove a harmless substitute for a glass of sherry, or a little drop of cold brandy-and-water, or a glass of beer, as the case may be.

Gruel is a compound which I would despair of making palatable; nevertheless, fortunately all palates are not alike. A table-spoonful of groats—or, as I believe they are pronounced, grits—must be mixed in a little cold water, and worked smooth with a spoon. About a pint of boiling water must then be poured on them, and the whole quantity boiled gently and stirred over a clear fire for about a quarter of an hour. Gruel can, of course, be made with milk, or flavoured in a variety of ways. For a bad cold, a table-spoonful of treacle is sometimes serviceable, or a little sweet spirit of nitre, or a table-spoonful of rum, a little sugar being of course added.

As a rule, in cooking for *real* invalids, the aim

should be nourishment combined with the greatest simplicity of flavour. There are, however, of course, many cases where the palate has to be tickled, while at the same time the digestion has to be consulted. In these cases the cook's art is often put to the test. In many cases of diseases that may be termed wasting, really rich but, at the same time, light dishes are requisite. We would instance sweetbreads, stewed oysters, calves' brains, lambs' tails, &c.; but to enter into an elaborate account of the proper method of preparing such delicacies would be out of place in an article on invalid food, which is of necessity cursory.

Objections have, however, ofttimes been made to cookery as an art, when the object in view has been simply to stir up the jaded appetite in the overfed, whose proper treatment would be in accordance with the famous advice of Abernethy to the dyspeptic alderman—viz., "Live on a shilling a day, and earn it." When, however, our object is to alleviate those who suffer from disease, and who loathe food unless brought to them in a palatable form, even those who lead lives that may be termed severely simple will admit, skill in the preparation of food may at times vie with, and even excel, skill in the preparation of drugs.

INDEX.

	PAGE		PAGE
Acetic Acid, Uses of.	64	Celery Sauce	189
Adaptation of Dinner to Guest..	86	Chicken Broth.	247
		,, Salads	135
Arrangement of Table	49, 94	,, Cutlets	86
Arrowroot.	246	Chops, Greasy.	19
Asparagus Salad	132	,, To Grill.	20
Aspic Jelly.	87	Champagne-cup	155
Balls, Stuffing	178	Christmas Cheer	201
Bashawed Lobster	146	,, Dinner	191
Beef, Roast	196	,, Pudding	193
Beef-tea	243	Claret-cup	142, 152, 153
Bloaters	73	Claret, Mulled	204
Bishop, Bowl of	202	Coffee, How to Make	78
Books, Cookery	11	Coriander-seeds, Uses of	101
Bread-and-Milk	251	Copper, Dangerous Properties of	109
Bread-crumbs, Fried.	169		
Bread-raspings, Uses of	14	Curry	118, 123, 226
Breakfast Dishes	68	,, Sauce	226
Brown Thickening	119	Curried Sweetbreads.	118
Butter, Lobster.	25	,, Mutton	121
,, Melted	33	,, Shrimps	232
Cake, Wedding	236	Cutlets, Chicken	86
,, Almond Paste for	237	,, Lobster	25, 227
,, Icing for	237	Cucumber, How to Dress.	141
Camellias from Turnips	97	Devil Sauce	36

	PAGE
Dinner à la Russe	82, 85
Dinners, Expense of old-fashioned	82, 85
Dinner, How to Give a Nice Little	79
Dishes, How to Make Look Nice	56
Dyspepsia, Causes of	77
Early Rising, Importance of	71
Economy	22
Eels, Stewed	225
,, Souchet	144, 216, 228
,, Fried	228
Egg and Bread-crumb, To	13
Eggs and Bacon	73
Expenses of Dinners Compared	85
Extravagancies of the Table	32
Fat, Preservation of Frying	18
Filters, Importance of	158
Fish Dinners	221
Fish, How to get Cheap	39
,, Grilled for Breakfast	76
Flounders, Fried	228
,, Souchet	144, 228
Flowers for Table	83, 94
Forcemeat for Larks	90
Forks, Relays of	224
Food for Invalids	247
Fry, To	12
Fried Bread-crumbs	169
Frying-pan, Uses and Abuses of	1, 11
Game and Gravy	160
,, Salmi of	169
Glaze	95
Goose, Roast	161, 198
Golden-colour, To fry	12
Gravy	106
,, for Lamb	108
,, ,, Game	169
Groseille	152
Grouse, Roast	165
Gruel	251
Ham, Potted	38
,, and Eggs	72
Ham, To Decorate	98
Hare, How to Cook	171
,, Roast	172
Hare, Jugged	177
,, Soup	179
Horseradish Sauce	206
Invalids, Food for	247
Irish Stew	187
Jelly	101
,, Aspic	87
Jugged Hare	177
Kidneys	76
Kitchen Economy	22
Kromeskies, Russian	35
Lamb, How to Roast	106

INDEX.

	PAGE
Larks	90, 91
Lemonade	251
,, Home-made	157
Lettuce, To dry	130
Lobster, Bashawed	146
,, Salad	60, 135
,, Sauce	23
,, Butter	25
,, Cutlets	27, 227
Loin of Mutton	35
Luxury, Increase of	127
Mayonnaise Sauce	63, 135
Mince for Invalids	247
Mince-meat	197
Mince with poached Eggs	47
Mint Sauce	110
Mock-turtle Soup, Pig's Head	39
Mullet, Red, *en papillote*	227
Mushrooms *au gratin*	144
Mutton, Loin of	35
,, Cold Leg of	43
,, Curried	121
Oil, English Prejudice against	124
Ornaments for Lobster Salad	64
,, Variety of	66
Paper Cases for Larks	90
Parsley, To fry	17
Partridge, Red-legged	162

	PAGE
Partridge, Roast	165
Peas, Green	108
Pea Soup	184
Picnic Dainties	138
Pig, Roast, Indian Method	23
Pigs' Heads for Mock Turtle	39
Pigeon Pie	141
Pine-apple Syrup	142
Potatoes, New and Old	110
Potato Salad	133
Polled Ham	38
Pudding, Corn-flour	100
,, Plum	193
Red Mullet	227
Recipes, Extravagance of	21
Rissoles	46, 90
Rice for Curry	122
Russian Kromeskies	35
Salad, Mayonnaise	59, 135
,, Lobster	60, 135
,, Asparagus	132
,, Potato	132
Salads, and how to make them	124, 127
Salads, ordinary Method	129
,, Mixed English	133
,, Vegetable, Cold	134
,, Chicken	135
,, Salmon	135
Sauce, Bread	167

	PAGE		PAGE
Sauce, Devil	36	Spring Dishes	104
,, Lobster	23, 112	Stew, Irish	187
,, Mint	110	Stew-pans, Power of retaining Heat	120
,, Celery	189		
,, Shrimp	112	Stock from Leg of Mutton	46
,, Horseradish	206	,, Good	214
,, Tartare	113	Stuffing, Chestnut	207
,, Curry	118	,, Veal	174
Salmon Salad	135	,, Balls	178
,, and Pickle Sauce	225	Supper, How to Give a	93
,, How to Boil	111	Sweetbread, Fried	12, 18
,, ,, ,, Carve	112	Table Arrangement	49
,, Grilled	112	Tea, Beef-	243
Salmi of Game	168	Toast-and-Water	249
Sandwiches	99	Trifle	102
Sausages	74, 75	Turkey, To Utilise a Cold	35
Sausage-machine	74	,, To Glaze a	95
Savoury Summer Dishes	114	Turnips for Flowers	97
Servants' Stupidity	30	Turtle Soup	209
,, Extravagance	29	,, Flesh, Dried	213
Soup, Hare	179	Veal Stuffing	174
,, Vermicelli	51	Uses and Abuses of a Frying-pan	1
,, Mock-turtle	39		
,, Pea	184	Wassail-Bowl	205
,, Turtle	209	Wedding Breakfasts	233
Smelts, Fried	228	,, Bill of Fare for	233
Shrimps, Curried	232	,, Cake	236
Sole, Fried	13	Whitebait	230
Soda, Carbonate, for softening Water	110	Whiting, Fried	221
		White of Eggs, To Utilise	102

CASSELL PETTER & GALPIN, BELLE SAUVAGE WORKS, LONDON, E.C.

A SELECTION FROM

Cassell Petter & Galpin's Publications.

The Great Painters of Christendom, from Cimabue to Wilkie. By JOHN FORBES ROBERTSON. Illustrated throughout with carefully-executed Engravings of the Masterpieces of the several Painters. Royal 4to, cloth elegant, gilt edges, £3 3s.

Picturesque Europe. Vols. I. and II., comprising *The British Isles*, complete. Each Volume contains Thirteen exquisite Steel Plates from Original Drawings, and about 200 Original Illustrations. With Descriptive Letterpress. Royal 4to, 300 pages, cloth gilt, gilt edges, £2 2s. each; morocco, £6 6s. each.
The Two Volumes can also be obtained bound together in one Volume.

The Royal Academy Album 1877. Consisting of a Series of Permanent Photographs from the Choicest Works of Art in the Royal Academy of 1877. Edited by SAMUEL JENNINGS, F.L.S. Handsome 4to, cloth, gilt edges, £3 3s.

Royal Quarto Shakespeare. Edited by CHARLES and MARY COWDEN CLARKE, and containing about 600 Illustrations by H. C. SELOUS. Printed in new large type on royal 4to paper. Complete in Three Vols., cloth gilt, gilt edges, £3 3s.; morocco, £6 6s.

The Leopold Shakspere. Dedicated, by permission, to H.R.H. Prince Leopold. The Text of the Leopold Shakspere is that of Professor DELIUS, while an Introduction to the entire Work has been written by Mr. F. J. FURNIVALL. This Edition includes "The Two Noble Kinsmen" and "Edward III." With about 400 Illustrations. Small 4to, 1,184 pages, cloth, 10s. 6d.

The National Portrait Gallery. Complete in Four Volumes. Each containing Twenty Portraits of our most distinguished Celebrities, printed in the highest style of Chromo-Lithography, with accompanying Memoirs, compiled from Authentic Sources. Cloth, 12s. 6d. each.

The Races of Mankind. By ROBERT BROWN, M.A., F.R.G.S., &c. With 500 Illustrations. Complete in Four Vols., extra crown 4to, cloth, 6s. each; or in Two Vols., cloth, £1 1s.

The Countries of the World. By Dr. ROBERT BROWN, M.A., F.R.G.S., &c. Vol. I., with about 140 Illustrations and Maps, extra crown 4to, cloth, 6s.

Cookery, Cassell's Dictionary of. With numerous Engravings and full-page Coloured Plates. Containing about 9,000 Recipes. 1,180 pages, royal 8vo, cloth, 15s.

Cassell Petter & Galpin: London, Paris and New York.

3G—1077

Turkey in Europe. By LIEUT.-COL. JAMES BAKER. With Maps. Demy 8vo, cloth, 21s.

Egypt as it Is. By J. C. McCOAN, late Editor of the "Levant Herald." Demy 8vo, cloth, with Map, 21s.

Russia. By D. MACKENZIE WALLACE, M.A. An account of the Political, Social, and Domestic Life of the Russian People. Two Vols., cloth, 24s.

A Ride to Khiva. By CAPTAIN BURNABY. With large Maps showing Districts Traversed. *Cheap Edition*, cloth, 7s. 6d.

England, Cassell's Illustrated History of, from the Earliest Period to the Present Time. With about 2,000 Illustrations. NEW TONED PAPER EDITION. Complete in Nine Vols., cloth, each, 9s. LIBRARY EDITION, bound in brown cloth, gilt tops, £4 10s.

Old and New London. Vols. I., II., III., IV., and V. now ready, with about 200 Illustrations in each. Extra crown 4to, cloth gilt, 9s. each. (*To be completed in Six Vols.*)

Protestantism, The History of. By the Rev. J. A. WYLIE, LL.D. Complete in Three Vols., with upwards of 200 Original Illustrations in each. Extra crown 4to, cloth, 9s. each.

United States, Cassell's History of the. Complete in Three Vols., with 200 Illustrations and Maps in each Vol. Extra crown 4to, cloth, 9s. each.

India, Cassell's History of. With Maps, Plans, and Illustrations. Complete in Two Vols. Extra crown 4to, 576 pages, cloth, 9s. each.

Popular Educator, Cassell's New. Revised to the Present Date, with numerous Additions. Complete in Six Vols., 412 pp. each, cloth, 6s. each ; or Three Vols., half-calf, £2 10s.

Technical Educator, Cassell's. With Coloured Designs and numerous Illustrations. Complete in Four Vols., extra crown 4to, cloth, 6s. each ; or Two Vols., half-calf, 31s. 6d.

Bible Educator, The. Edited by the Rev. E. H. PLUMPTRE, D.D., assisted by some of the most eminent Scholars and Divines. With 400 Engravings and Maps. Complete in Four Vols., cloth, 6s. each ; or in Two Double Vols., 21s.

The Life of Christ. By the Rev. Canon FARRAR, D.D., F.R.S. Complete in Two Volumes, cloth, 24s. ; morocco, £2 2s.

The Half-Guinea Illustrated Bible. Containing nearly 1,000 Original Illustrations specially executed for this Edition from Original Photographs and other authentic sources. Printed in clear readable type, with References. Crown 4to. Strongly bound in cloth, 10s. 6d.

The Child's Bible. With 220 Illustrations. Demy 4to, cloth gilt, £1 1s. ; leather, 30s. ; morocco elegant, 42s.

Cassell Petter & Galpin: London, Paris and New York.

A Selection from Cassell Petter & Galpin's Publications (continued). 3

At the South Pole. A New Story. By W. H. G. KINGSTON. With Forty Engravings. Crown 8vo, gilt edges, 5s.

Civil Service, Guide to Employment in the. With an Introduction by J. D. MORELL, LL.D. Cloth, 2s. 6d.

Common-sense Housekeeping. By PHILLIS BROWNE. With Illustrations. Extra fcap. 8vo, 250 pages, cloth, 2s. 6d.

Common-sense Cookery. By A. G. PAYNE. With Illustrations. 256 pages, extra fcap. 8vo, cloth, 2s. 6d.

Dictionary of Phrase and Fable; giving the Derivation, Source, or Origin of Common Phrases, Allusions, and Words that have a Tale to Tell. By the Rev. Dr. BREWER. 1,000 pages, cloth, 7s. 6d.

Dictionary of English Literature. Being a Comprehensive Guide to English Authors and their Works. By W. DAVENPORT ADAMS. 720 pages, extra fcap. 4to, cloth, 15s.

Dog, The. By IDSTONE. With Twelve Illustrations by G. EARL. Cloth, 2s. 6d.

Esther West. By ISA CRAIG-KNOX. Illustrated with Twenty-four Engravings. Imperial 16mo. Cloth, gilt edges, 5s.

Facts and Hints for Every-day Life. A Comprehensive Book on Every subject connected with the Comforts of Home and the Health and Prosperity of its Inmates. 2s. 6d.

Golden Days. By JEANIE HERING. The Experiences of an English Girl's School Life in Germany. Cloth, gilt edges, 5s.

Half-Hours with Early Explorers. By T. FROST. Profusely Illustrated. Cloth, 5s.

Historical Scenes. Containing some of the most striking Episodes from History. Selected by E. SPOONER. Cloth, 2s. 6d.

How to Get On. Edited by GODFREY GOLDING. With 1,000 Precepts for Practice. Cloth bevelled, gilt edges, 3s. 6d.

Manners of Modern Society. A Comprehensive Work on the Etiquette of the Present Day. Cloth gilt, 2s. 6d.

North-West Passage by Land. By Viscount MILTON and Dr. CHEADLE. *Original Edition*, demy 8vo, with Twenty-two Plates, 21s. *Cheap Edition*, crown 8vo, cloth, 2s. 6d. ; gilt edges, 3s. 6d.

Notable Shipwrecks. By UNCLE HARDY. Crown 8vo, 320 pages, with Frontispiece. Cloth gilt, 5s.

Our Children, and How to Rear and Train Them. A Manual for Parents, in the Physical, Educational, Religious, and Moral Training of their Children. Crown 8vo, cloth, 3s. 6d.

Pictures of School Life and Boyhood. Selected from the Best Authors, and Edited by PERCY FITZGERALD, M.A. Cloth, gilt edges, 3s. 6d.

Cassell Petter & Galpin : London, Paris and New York.

4 *A Selection from Cassell Petter & Galpin's Publications (continued).*

Practical Kennel Guide, The. By Dr. GORDON STABLES. With Illustrations. Crown 8vo, 204 pages, cloth, 3s. 6d.

Practical Poultry-Keeper, The. By L. WRIGHT. With Forty-eight Plain Illustrations. Cloth, 3s. 6d.; or with Thirty-six Plain Illustrations, and Eight new Chromo Plates, 5s.

Soldier and Patriot. The Story of GEORGE WASHINGTON. By F. M. OWEN. Cloth, bevelled boards, gilt edges, 256 pages, 3s. 6d.

Stories of Girlhood; or, The Brook and the River. A Book for Girls. By SARAH DOUDNEY. Illustrated. Extra fcap. 4to, cloth gilt, gilt edges, 5s.

Talks about Trees. A Popular Account of their Nature and Uses. By M. and E. KIRBY. Profusely Illustrated. Extra crown 8vo, 320 pages. Cloth, gilt edges, 3s. 6d.

The True Glory of Woman. By the Rev. Dr. LANDELS. Crown 8vo, cloth, gilt edges, 3s. 6d.

The Story of Captain Cook. By M. Jones. Illustrated with about Forty Engravings. Cloth, gilt edges, 5s.

The Three Homes. A Tale for Fathers and Sons. By F. T. L. HOPE. Crown 8vo, 400 pages, cloth, gilt edges, 5s.

The Theory and Action of the Steam Engine: for Practical Men. By W. H. NORTHCOTT, C.E. Demy 8vo, 224 pages, with numerous Diagrams and Tables, cloth, 7s. 6d.

Truth will Out. By JEANIE HERING, Author of "Golden Days," &c. Crown 8vo, 240 pages, cloth, gilt edges, 3s. 6d.

Wonders, Library of. A Series of Books for Boys. All Profusely Illustrated, and bound in cloth gilt, gilt edges, 3s. 6d. each.

Wonders of Animal Instinct.	Wonders of Architecture.
Wonders of Bodily Strength and Skill.	Wonderful Adventures.
Wonders of Acoustics.	Wonderful Balloon Ascents.
Wonders of Water.	Wonderful Escapes.

Working to Win. By MAGGIE SYMINGTON. With Four full-page Illustrations. Cloth, gilt edges, 5s.

Young Man in the Battle of Life, The. By the Rev. Dr. LANDELS. Fcap. 8vo, 292 pages. Cloth gilt, 3s. 6d.

CASSELL'S COMPLETE CATALOGUE, containing a complete List of Works, including Bibles and Religious Literature, Children's Books, Dictionaries, Educational Works, Fine Art Volumes, Handbooks and Guides, History, Miscellaneous, Natural History, Poetry, Travels, Serials.

Cassell Petter & Galpin: London, Paris and New York.

www.ingramcontent.com/pod-product-compliance
Lightning Source LLC
Chambersburg PA
CBHW021349230426
43666CB00006B/457